Incorporation

C.G.T. Canadian Legal Forms Ltd
Burnaby, B.C. / service@CanadaForms.com

NOTICE:

THIS PRODUCT IS NOT INTENDED TO PROVIDE LEGAL ADVICE. IT CONTAINS GENERAL INFORMATION FOR EDUCATIONAL PURPOSES ONLY. PLEASE CONSULT A LAWYER ABOUT ALL LEGAL MATTERS. THIS PRODUCT WAS NOT NECESSARILY PREPARED BY A PERSON LICENSED TO PRACTICE LAW IN YOUR PROVINCE.

Incorporation
© Copyright 2001 C.G.T. Canadian Legal Forms LTD
P.O. Box 82664
Burnaby, B.C. V5C 5W4
service@CanadaForms.com

1 2 3 4 5 6 7 8 9 10

This publication is designed to provide accurate and authoritative information in regard to subject matter covered. It is sold with the understanding that neither the publisher nor author is engaged in rendering legal, accounting, or other professional services. If legal advice or other expert assistance is required, the services of a competent professional should be sought.

Incorporation

Table of contents

Introduction
to
Incorporation

Millions of Canadians choose to incorporate their business each year. Whether you convert your present business or incorporate a start-up venture, *Incorporation* guides you through the incorporation process.

Once you have decided that the corporation is the correct form of organization for your business, you must go through the legal steps required to create your corporation. These steps vary for the federally incorporated entity as well as from province to province, and they also vary in complexity. But with careful planning, you can organize you own corporation—clearly, conveniently, and without costly legal fees.

Using the forms which generally conform to the legal requirements of the provinces (although it may be necessary to obtain additional province-specific forms from your provincial government) and information in this guide, you may incorporate in any province without a lawyer, and conduct meetings, record minutes, and protect your personal assets from business debts.

Now anyone may also incorporate a business under federal regulations with a minimum of headaches and legal fees—in this guide, we've made it E-Z!

The business entity

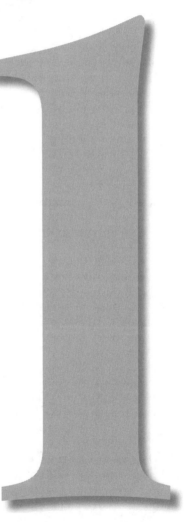

The business entity

Perhaps you've got a great idea for a new business. Maybe you're tired of working for other people and you want to be your own boss. Or maybe you've always dreamed of opening that sporting goods shop, or selling your arts and crafts, and you now have the money—or just the guts—to finally do it.

Once you are ready to start the ball rolling, there are so many things to consider! What kind of business, where you should locate, and where you'll get the money from. But even if you already know these answers, you still have one of the most important decisions to make about your new business—what form of business should it be?

note There are several kinds of businesses, each with its own variations, that you can choose from. Each has distinct advantages and disadvantages over the others, and each one fits a particular set of needs.

By what form of business, we don't mean whether you should open a bakery or a dance studio, but rather what legal form of business to choose. Aside from things like permits and employee contracts, you first need to choose a type of business entity the government will acknowledge (meaning, for the most part, whom Revenue Canada will acknowledge).

Choosing the right type of business

Before starting your business you must carefully consider which type of business entity will best suit your present and future needs.

The four basic business entities are:

1) individual or sole proprietorship

2) partnership

3) corporation

4) cooperative

Each offers its own unique advantages and disadvantages in regard to:

- liability and personal exposure

- costs, including filing fees and tax considerations

- the available methods of raising capital

- the time and costs of conversion

- the ability to attract and keep key personnel through fringe benefits or participations such as stock options

Examine the following types of business entities to find the right one for your needs—and your new business.

The sole proprietorship

The *sole proprietorship* is a business owned by an individual who is solely responsible for all aspects of the business. The owner is personally responsible for all debts of the business,

> **note** The sole proprietorship is the simplest form of business organization.

even in excess of the amount invested. For example, the sole proprietor business you have painstakingly built over the past 15 years is now suffering a financial slump. Your business shows a net worth of $100,000, but has amassed $175,000 in liabilities. If you close or dissolve your business, you are still be responsible for the additional $75,000 excess liabilities over net worth. The business and its owner are thus considered the same entity.

The advantages of a sole proprietorship include:

- Low start-up costs—legal and filing fees are minimal. However, many provinces and cities require at least a filing with the clerk, especially if using a fictitious or "doing business as" (DBA) name.

- Greatest freedom from regulation and paperwork

- Owner is in direct control with no interference from other owners.

- Taxes may be lower than with corporations.

The disadvantages include:

- Unlimited liability. The proprietor is responsible for the full amount of business debts no matter how incurred, which means that the proprietor's personal property may be taken to cover debts of the business. This, of course, is a significant disadvantage.

- Unstable business life since the sole owner's death or illness would terminate the business.

- Difficulty in raising additional capital or obtaining long-term financing because you cannot readily sell an ownership interest in a sole proprietorship.

The partnership

As with the sole proprietorship, the owners (partners) are personally liable for all the debts of the firm—unless a limited partnership is set up. Limited partnerships are complex legal structures where at least one partner, known as the general partner, must still have unlimited liability. In some cases, agreements for regular partnerships can become quite complex.

> *note* The *partnership* is a legal entity which is jointly owned by two or more individuals (although in some cases a partner may also be corporations or other type entities).

The advantages of a partnership include:

- Low start-up costs, since there usually are fewer filing fees and franchise taxes

- A broader management base than a sole proprietorship, and a more flexible management structure than a corporation

- Possible tax advantages, since a partnership avoids the double taxation of corporations, and because income can be taxed at personal income rates. Naturally, the personal income situations of the partners could also make this a disadvantage.

- Additional sources of capital and leverage by adding limited and special partners

- The duration of the entity can be limited to a stated time, or can continue indefinitely by amendment.

Chapter 1

The disadvantages include:

- Unlimited liability of at least one partner (in a limited partnership) and possibly all partners (in a regular partnership). The personal assets of the general partners are available to satisfy partnership debts.

- The life of a partnership is unstable, since the addition or departure of any of the partners causes the partnership to terminate.

- Obtaining large sums of capital is relatively difficult, as the financing cannot be obtained from the public through a stock offering.

- The acts of just one partner, even unauthorized acts—clandestine or otherwise—can bind all the partners.

- An individual partnership interest cannot be sold or transferred.

- Most tax-supported fringe benefits, such as pension and profit-sharing arrangements, are unavailable to partnerships.

The corporation

The *corporation* is a legally endowed entity with rights and responsibilities, and has a life of its own—independent of the owners and operators. It is regarded as a distinct and independent entity—separate from its owners.

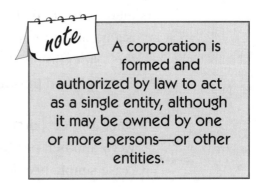

note

A corporation is formed and authorized by law to act as a single entity, although it may be owned by one or more persons—or other entities.

The advantages of a corporation include:

- Limited liability. The owners are not personally liable for debts and obligations of the corporation. They personally lose only to the extent of their investment into the corporation—with the exception that they can become personally liable for certain types of taxes, such as payroll taxes withheld

Limited liability is one major reason so many businesses become incorporated.

from the employees' paycheques but not paid to Revenue Canada and/or provincial taxing authorities. If the business fails or loses a lawsuit claim against it, the general creditors cannot attach the owners' (shareholders') homes, cars, or other personal property.

• Capital can be raised more easily than under other forms of ownership. This does not mean, however, that a new corporation can easily sell shares of stock to the public. The sale of stock is highly regulated by both federal and provincial governments, and obtaining bank loans for a fledgling business may be no easier for a corporation than for a partnership or proprietorship.

• Ownership in a corporation is more readily transferrable, including transferring shares to family members—as well as selling your interest to another person. However, in many small corporations it is advisable to put restrictions on the transfer of shares especially if the stockholders must work together. This is generally accomplished through stockholder agreements.

• Since the corporation is an independent legal entity (just as if it were another person), it has a continuous existence. It does not cease simply because one of the shareholders dies or retires.

• A corporation has a defined, centralized management. Control rests in the board of directors, and its powers are exercised through the elected officers of the corporation.

• Many retail companies offer substantial discounts—such as travel— to corporations

- Retirement funds, defined-contribution plans, money-purchase plans, and other profit-sharing, pension, and stock option plans may be more easily set up with a corporation.

The disadvantages include:

- Corporations are subject to more governmental regulation than either partnerships or sole proprietorships.

- Corporations are the most expensive form of business to organize.

- Corporations suffer double taxation, since both the corporate entity and its individual owners have to file tax returns.

- Record-keeping requirements are more extensive and detailed with a corporation.

- Operating across provincial lines often becomes complicated because corporations need to "qualify to do business" in provinces where they are not incorporated. This is explained later in detail.

- Ending the corporate existence, and in many cases even changing the structure of the organization, can be more complicated and certainly more costly than for partnerships and proprietorships.

In the province of British Columbia, the *British Columbia Company Act* empowers a special category of corporations called a "special liability company" or the *non-personal liability company.*

Under the *Company Act*, the NPL is restricted to high-risk ventures such as the exploration for, mining of, or production of minerals, coal, petroleum, or natural gases. Also, the NPL may sell par-value shares (see Chapter 4 - Corporate stock) at a greater discount than a regular company (where discounts are limited to 25%).

New companies incorporating under the NPL rules do so in hopes of raising enough capital to carry on or expand their exploration program. They are able to accomplish this by "floating" or issuing additional stock. This somewhat popular method of securing additional funding employs the selling of heavily-discounted (cheap) stock in large blocks to big time investors—who in turn will resell the stock at substantially higher prices.

This creates a pyramid effect in the stock distribution equation. With this type of funding, directors of NPLs will usually extend the 14-day grace period required between ordering the stock and paying for it, to a 60-day grace period allowing the big investors to resell the stock without ever actually having paid for it.

The British Columbia regulations governing incorporation of a specially limited or NPL company are the same as for a regular company with the following exceptions:

- The letters "NPL" **must** be displayed whenever the company name is used or displayed, including use in advertisements, name plates, or correspondence.

- The name of an NPL company **must** include the words "non-personal liability" or the abbreviation "NPL."

- An NPL company is restricted in its financial dealings. It cannot lend money or guarantee (co-sign) the debts of another person or corporation. It also cannot finance or help finance another person or business entity.

Due to this exclusive and limited nature, more and more lawyers are not recommending the use of NPL companies—even to mining and oil or gas companies.

The cooperative

A *cooperative* is a special type of corporation which is organized, owned and controlled by members who join together for a common benefit. Cooperatives differ from ordinary corporations under these six guiding principles:

1) Membership is voluntary and open to anyone.

2) Each member has one vote no matter how many shares are held.

3) Return on investment is limited by legislation.

4) Surplus earnings are returned to members.

5) Education is provided.

6) Cooperatives act in cooperation with other co-ops.

The advantages of a cooperative are:

- Owned and controlled by members.

- Democratic control—"one member, one vote."

- Limited liability.

- Profit distribution (surplus earnings) to members in proportion to use of service; surplus may be allocated in shares or cash.

Disadvantages of a cooperative are:

- Possibility of development of conflict between members.

- Longer decision making process.

- Requires members to participate to achieve success.

- Extensive record keeping is necessary.

- Less incentive to invest additional capital.

Cooperatives intending to operate in more than one province can be incorporated under the *Canada Cooperatives Act*.

Should you incorporate your business?

The demands of running a business often prevent business owners from taking time to carefully consider their options, assess their situations, and effectively plan their future. Even if you are not yet in business but are planning to start a new enterprise, you must first decide on the best form of organization. Whether to incorporate or to conduct a business in some other form—a sole proprietorship or a partnership—involves many considerations.

Your decision on the form of organization for your business should be decided with great consideration to all of the advantages and disadvantages. However, the prevailing attitude is that a corporation is the preferred form of organization, since its advantages far outweigh its disadvantages.

Once you have decided that incorporation is the correct form of organization for your business, you must go through the legal steps required to create your corporation in an orderly procedure. These steps vary in complexity from province to province. With careful planning, most people can easily organize their own corporation without a lawyer, thus saving hundreds of dollars in legal fees.

Incorporate before you incur liabilities

Many business owners start their ventures as unincorporated sole proprietorships. Concern about losing personal assets arises only when their business heads toward bankruptcy. If you are that business owner, you may possibly still escape personal liability for your business' obligations, but only if you quickly incorporate your business and transfer proprietorship business assets to the corporation. The corporation should then pay first the oldest business obligations. These would be the proprietorship obligations for which you are personally liable. As your corporation pays these older debts, it will incur newer debts with the same or other suppliers. However, these debts will now be corporate obligations. Your goal is to fully pay all the proprietorship debts and only then can you safely liquidate your business—when its creditors have no personal recourse against you or your personal assets.

This strategy demands careful coordination and open disclosure. For instance, you must operate your business until you fully pay all pre-incorporation debts. You must also advise creditors that your business is now incorporated. Finally, your creditors must apply your payments to the proprietorship debts that you want discharged. Earmark on each check how it is to be applied.

> If you now operate an unincorporated business, convert before you get into serious financial trouble. Your smartest strategy is to incorporate before starting your business.

Eight ways to lose corporate protection

Your corporation can be an effective liability insulator only if it functions as a corporation. You can lose your corporate protection through one of eight common mistakes that allow creditors to pierce the corporate veil and sue you personally for the corporate debts.

The eight mistakes are:

1) **Commingling funds:** Operate your corporation as a distinct entity, separate from yourself in every respect. Segregate corporate funds from your own. Document funds transferred between you and your corporation. Example: Are your funds invested in the corporation as a loan or a contribution to capital? Conversely, are funds you take from the corporation a loan, dividends, salary or expense reimbursement? Record every transaction on both your personal and corporate records, and similarly record all financial transactions between related corporations or entities.

2) **Commingling assets:** The prohibitions against commingled cash also apply to other assets, such as inventory. You can safely transfer inventory between corporations, provided you maintain accurate records. Creditors of a corporation can throw affiliated corporations into bankruptcy when they encounter undocumented transactions between the bankrupt corporation and its affiliates.

3) **Not signing documents as a corporate agent:** If you operate as a corporation, have its legal documents say so. Clearly state the corporate name and designate your title near your signature on all documents and checks.

4) **Not operating your corporations autonomously:** Operate multiple corporations autonomously. For instance, use separate not

identical or interlocking boards of directors. Officers of related corporations should occupy different positions. Conduct separate corporate meetings and maintain separate corporate books.

5) **Failing to keep adequate corporate records:** Creditors can challenge the corporate existence when records improperly document key corporate actions. Keep good records for all director and stockholder meetings.

6) **Failing to identify your business as a corporation:** Creditors must realize that they are dealing with a corporation if you are to avoid personal lawsuits from creditors and others who may think it is a proprietorship or partnership. Your corporate name should be on all signs, letterheads, bill-heads, checks and wherever else your business name appears.

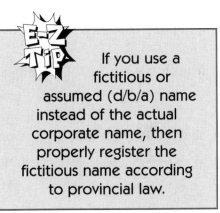

If you use a fictitious or assumed (d/b/a) name instead of the actual corporate name, then properly register the fictitious name according to provincial law.

7) **Operating a dissolved corporation:** A corporation dissolved by the provincial or federal government has its corporate protection voided. Pay corporate taxes and franchise fees so your corporation remains in good standing. And never voluntarily dissolve a corporation with debts. These debts then automatically become your own as its stockholder.

8) **Undercapitalizing your corporation:** Too small an investment in your corporation, or too little paid for its shares of stock compared to what you loaned your corporation, can spell trouble. There's no conclusively safe ratio, but most lawyers and accountants recommend that at least $1 should be invested as equity (for shares) for every $4 in loans.

When operating your corporation, apply five more creditor-proofing tests:

1) Does your corporation have a business address and telephone number?

2) Do you have canceled corporate checks to show that the corporation pays its own expenses?

3) Have all necessary business licenses been issued to the corporation?

4) Does your corporation maintain bank accounts?

5) Does your corporation transact significant business with unaffiliated parties?

Each point can help establish that your corporation is engaged in business as a legitimate entity, and one separate and apart from you as its owner.

Creditors frequently try to pierce the corporate veil and claim that the corporation is nothing more than a sham alter-ego of its principals. But a creditor has the burden of proof. While courts seldom dismiss the corporation's important protection, they will do so if its owners flagrantly ignore these or other basic requirements for properly maintaining their corporation as a distinct entity.

A creditor's personal lawsuit against a corporate owner is most frequently only another bad faith maneuver to force the owner to defend the suit or settle. Countersue the creditor and his lawyer for frivolous, bad faith litigation should this happen to you. Corporate protection does not guarantee that you will not need to personally defend against a bad faith creditor claim, but you will keep your personal assets safe by observing these points.

Where to incorporate?

2

Where to incorporate?

Companies with an intention to carry on business in more than one province or in foreign countries may prefer to incorporate under Canadian federal law. This permits the company to carry on business in all of the provinces in Canada without being licensed by that province, although registration may still be required.

The first issue to decide is the province within which to organize your corporation. Most businesses incorporate in the province where they are located. However, there are some advantages to incorporating federally.

> *note* A business can be incorporated through either the federal government or a provincial government.

Federal vs. provincial incorporation

The benefits of registering your corporation under federal jurisdiction are two-fold. First, you may conduct business in any province or territory throughout Canada subject to extra-provincial registration. Extra-provincial registration must be applied for when a corporation carries on business in a province other than the province in which it was incorporated. Secondly, because of the depth of the federal NUANS name search, your corporate name cannot be refused when registering in a province. Thus, with federal incorporation you gain added name protection. However, registering provincially is less expensive.

Base your decision on these important factors:

- the location of your physical facilities

- the cost of incorporating in a particular province

- the cost of becoming incorporated federally

- annual fees, and provincial and local taxes

- the laws governing corporations in that province

If you incorporate federally, what will it cost to be authorized to do business? This cost includes:

- fees to check and reserve the name you want to use for your corporation

- the cost of filing incorporation papers, and

- whether there is a one-time organizational fee or franchise tax (often based upon the number of shares authorized for the corporation to issue)

In addition to the initial incorporating costs, determine how much annual fees are in the province(s) in which you are considering doing business:

- Is there an annual report to file?

- How much is the filing fee?

- Is there an annual franchise tax?

- Is there a provincial or local income tax, and if so, how is it determined?

Many of these issues vary from province to province. In almost all instances, however, it is advisable for a small business corporation to organize within the province where it is located and will be conducting business—unless there are plans to do business in other provinces. Even with forms included with this guide, you must become familiar with the appropriate provincial statutes before filing incorporation papers.

Once you have decided whether to incorporate federally or provincially, there is a great deal of free information available about how to set up that corporation, or for using incorporation services at minimal fees. These may be obtained from the appropriate governmental departments, or on the Internet. A list of contact addresses and telephone numbers of departments to contact in the provinces is contained in the back of this guide.

Federal incorporation

All persons wishing to incorporate their business at the federal level, and all corporations already in existence, are subject to the *Canada Business Corporations Act*. The Canada Business Corporations Act provides the legal framework for creating and governing federally registered corporations. The Act and Regulations specify the conditions that must be met in order to form, operate, and dissolve a legal federally registered corporation.

If you wish to form a corporation under federal law, you must initially file the following forms (in duplicate) and pay the appropriate filing fees:

Form 1 Articles of Incorporation

Form 3 Notice of Registered Office

Form 6 Notice of Directors

Filing fee payable to the Receiver General for Canada

NUANS federal name search report (a corporate name search to make certain your name is not already in use by another company) not more than 90 days old. Note that a NUANS search is not required when making an initial filing for a corporation number only.

After a corporation has been incorporated federally, it may be necessary to file a notice with the province(s) where the corporation will be conducting its operations. This is known as *extra-provincial registration*.

To carry on business in another province, a corporation—whether federal or provincial—must register under the specific laws of the new province. The appropriate provincial authority must be consulted to determine what documentation is needed. Extra-provincial registration is not required for federal corporations in Ontario. Federal or provincial corporations need not obtain a license to conduct business there.

The extra-provincial registration process simply involves completing the appropriate form and paying a fee. Approval is usually granted barring problems with the corporate name.

note Incorporating federally, and employing the federal NUANS name search eliminates the possibility of a name being refused provincially.

Schedule of fees

Certificate of Incorporation	$500.00
Certificate of Amendment	200.00
Restated Certificate of Incorporation	50.00
Certificate of Amalgamation	200.00
Certificate of Continuance	200.00

Letter of Satisfaction	$200.00
Certificate of Revival	200.00
Certificate of Revocation of Intent to Dissolve	50.00
Certificate of Compliance (or, known as a "Certificate of Good Standing")	10.00
Corrected Certificate (same fee as certificate it replaced)	
Sending the Annual Return to the Director	$50.00
Uncertified copies of documents (per page)	1.00
Certified copies of documents (per certificate)	35.00

Provincial incorporation

Take the following steps to incorporate provincially:

1) Name search. As with federal incorporation, the name must be searched through a search company using the NUANS system. Look in the Yellow Pages under "Searchers of Records."

2) If your company does not yet have a name, the next file number in the registration sequence is assigned to it. You must also choose to use *Corporation*, *Incorporation* or *Limited* (or its corresponding acronym) as a part of the corporate name form.

3) As with federal incorporation, the *Articles of Incorporation* are filed with the Ministry of Consumer and Commercial Relations. This form provides details, such as: corporation address, directors' names and addresses, basic company structure, types of shares, rights and restrictions on share types, and the number and value of the shares. Forms are available in many stationery stores or in appropriate Land Registry offices (see the Resources section of this guide).

4) Complete an *Initial Filing Notice* from the Ministry of Consumer and Commercial Relations. This form provides information about directors and officers of the corporation, i.e., president, vice-president, secretary and treasurer, as well as the location of the corporate records.

5) The corporation must then register as an employer with a Revenue Canada Taxation office to provide for Income Tax, Canada Pension Plan, Unemployment Insurance, and Worker's Compensation.

6) The corporation must file annual tax returns at both the provincial and federal level.

Extra-provincial registration

There may be additional factors affecting the decision of whether to incorporate federally or provincially. For example, public disclosure of all financial statements for larger private corporations, as well as public corporations, is required under the federal law. In certain provinces, such as Ontario, private corporations do not have to file their financial statements, except as a part of their tax returns, which are confidential.

Extra-provincial registration and fees

Province	Cost
Ontario	no cost for Canadian jurisdictions
Newfoundland The Registrar Registry of Companies P.O. Box 8700, Confederation Building, East Block, St. John's, Newfoundland A1B 4J6 (709) 729-3316	$260 - $560

Prince Edward Island (PEI) Corporations Division Department of Community Affairs Province of Prince Edward Island P.O. Box 2000 Charlottetown, P.E.I. C1A 7N8 (902) 368-4550	$200.00
Nova Scotia Registry of Joint Stock Companies P.O. Box 1529 Halifax, Nova Scotia B3J 2Y4 (902) 424-7770	$200.00
New Brunswick The Director Corporate Affairs Branch Department of Justice P.O. Box 6000 Fredericton, New Brunswick E3B 5H1 (506) 453-2703	$200.00
Manitoba Companies Office Room 1010 405 Broadway Winnipeg, Manitoba R3C 3L6 (204) 945-2500; (204) 945-5999	$250.00
Saskatchewan Corporations Branch 2nd Floor, 1871 Smith Street Regina, Saskatchewan S4P 3V9 (306) 787-2962	$250.00

Alberta	$300.00
Riverbend Registry	
Room 201	
596 Riverbend Square	
Edmonton, Alberta T6R 2E3	
(privatised registry office)	
(250) 356-8648	

Alberta $300.00
Riverbend Registry
Room 201
596 Riverbend Square
Edmonton, Alberta T6R 2E3
(privatised registry office)
(250) 356-8648

British Columbia $300.00
Registrar of Companies
940 Blanshard Street
Victoria, B.C. V8W 3E6
(250) 356-8648

Northwest Territories $300.00
Corporate Registrar
Dept. of Justice
Government of Northwest Territories,
Box 1320
Yellowknife, NT X1A 2L9
(867) 873-7492

Courier Address:
4903 49th Street
Courthouse, 3rd Floor
Yellowknife, NT X1A 2L9

Yukon Consumer and Commercial Services, $300.00
Corporate Affairs
Box 2703
Whitehorse, Yukon Y1A 2C6
(867) 667-5442

Establishing your corporation

3

Establishing your corporation

Once you have decided to set up your own corporation, you must select a corporate name and have it researched to see if the federal or provincial government in which you are going to incorporate will allow you to use it. Geographical names, such as lakes, mountains or cities can provide a unique title for corporate names as can types of trees, historical or mythological events. Businesses which deal directly with consumers often have less formal, more friendly names than business-to-business corporations. Choose a characteristic of the product for the consumer market.

> **note** Look for ideas from other sources when creating a distinctive corporate name.

Choosing your name

To make your choice of names acceptable to the Director, Companies Branch, you must consider the three specific components:

1) **A distinctive element:** The part of your corporate name which could be initials, numerals, a geographic location, a coined phrase, or even a contrived word.

2) **A descriptive element:** This part of your corporate identity must describe the type of business you are engaged in. A year could also

be used in the name, as long as it represents the year of incorporation or registration.

3) **A corporate designation:** The name of an incorporated business must end with "Corporation," "Incorporated," "Limited," "Corp.," "Inc.," or "Ltd," respectively.

Certain words used in corporate names will immediately set off whistles and bells in the Registrar's office—these should be avoided at all costs: words such as "Institute," "Condominium," or "Co-operative." Also to be avoided are names that imply connection to the Royal Family, the government, a branch of the military service, or any department of government.

Without saying so, the Registrar will refuse any name which appears to be obscene or vulgar in nature, and a name which reflects too broad a spectrum of goods, such as "General Motors" or "Best Foods."

Use of a number(s), instead of words, in a corporate name is allowed, but they must be the assigned corporate number. If you have not been assigned a number as yet, your corporation number will be assigned as the next available number by the Registrar's office.

Similar names can cause many business problems. Most provinces will not allow a name that is the same or "deceptively similar" to a name already on record in the province. For example, choosing XYZ Corp. may be a problem, even if your business will be a restaurant and the already existing XYZ Inc. is a bakery. It often helps to choose a proper name and a descriptive word. In the above example, choosing XYZ Restaurant Corp. or XYZ Foods Corp. might not be considered "deceptively similar" to the already established XYZ Inc.

> *note*
>
> You must investigate whether the name you want is already being used by someone else.

Reserving your corporate name

Reserving your choice of names (up to three at one time) is done by filing for a NUANS name search, paying the required fee, and waiting to receive clearance. In some cases you can check the availability of the name with a telephone call. Always make sure you clear the proposed corporate name before you prepare and file your corporate papers.

The two most important benefits from protecting your business name are:

1) reducing the probability of another business forcing you to change your corporate name after your business has become established

2) reducing the probability of another business, which started after your business, from retaining a name which is confusing with your name.

Name search

Regulations in the federal and most provincial jurisdictions of Canada require that a corporate name not be confused with an existing trade name or trade mark anywhere in Canada. However, the application of this regulation is quite different within each jurisdiction.

For example, Ontario is unlikely to refuse a proposed name unless it is virtually identical with an existing name. The government places the responsibility with the incorporator to determine confusion. In contrast, the federal government makes the determination of confusion for the incorporator. This results in the federal rejection of many corporate names that Ontario would allow.

Although a NUANS name search for incorporating an Ontario company contains corporate names across Canada, other provinces generally do not search Ontario trade names. This means that if you incorporate "ABC Enterprises Ltd." in Ontario, someone else could incorporate "ABC Enterprises Ltd." in another province—at a later date.

Additional protection may be obtained by registering a trademark on your corporate name. Registration of a trademark is valid for 15 years, at a cost of $150 per registration, through the Registrar of Trademarks, Industry Canada, Canadian Intellectual Property. If, and after the trademark has been allowed, an additional fee of $200 is required to actually register the

note Most provinces search the names of federal corporations, thus providing a greater degree of protection for your corporate name. However, provincial regulations will determine the degree of similarity permitted.

trademark. The Trademarks Act outlines what is or is not an acceptable form of trademark

Use of a trade name

Many businesses operate under a *trade name*. A trade name is not necessarily the same as the registered corporate name, such as Doe Importing Ltd. d/b/a Asian Treasures. The reasoning behind such a practice is that the trade name (or "doing business as") is oftentimes more easily associated with an established product and can be more readily advertised.

If you have registered and you use a name other than your corporate name, you are required to use both the corporate name and the trade name on all contracts, invoices, negotiable instruments, as well as orders for goods and services. In Ontario, for example, corporations that use trade names are required to register the names under which they conduct business with the Companies Branch, and such registration lasts for five years—subject to renewal.

For example, consider the proprietor or other type of entity who has a long-established business and clientele who rapidly associate with the trade name through advertising and good will (as in "Asian Treasures," above). When the proprietor incorporated "Doe Importing Ltd." and did not want to lose any name or prestige association due to the incorporation, he or she picked up its previous trade name of "Asian Treasures" as a d/b/a.

By filing a *Statement of Name Registration* with the respective province, you can retain the trade name and all of the prestige you have developed into that name. If you have not yet incorporated, this should also be reflected in your *Articles of Incorporation*.

Beginning the paperwork

After you have completed the name search and your choice of names (and or trademark) has been approved, you now begin the actual process of incorporation.

Prepare the Memorandum

note The Memorandum is your corporation's constitution.

Two copies of the Memorandum must be printed or typed on the prescribed form and submitted to the Registrar of Companies.

The Memorandum details the name of the corporation, its authorized capital, and the number of each class of shares acquired by the first stockholders (or subscribers). Both copies of the Memorandum must be signed by each of the subscribers.

In signing the Memorandum, each subscriber/shareholder assumes the duties and responsibilities as a director of the corporation until the first meeting of the shareholders is conducted. If and when new directors are elected, a Notice of Change of Directors (if a change occurs) must be filed.

Prepare your Articles of Incorporation

The *Articles of Incorporation* is the legal document which records the beginning of your corporation's history. If all of the information is properly documented and accepted by the Director of Companies Branch, a *Certificate of Incorporation* will then be issued—and thus your new corporation actually is born.

The Articles of Incorporation must include, in the following order:

1) **The corporate name.** This is the name you have chosen for your corporation and has been approved through a NUANS name search, a copy of which must be included.

2) **The registered office.** This is also known as the *address of service*, where provincial and federal governments may send you forms or contact you. This is where the original books of corporate records are kept. This address should be as detailed and accurate as possible, including such details as suite number, room, etc. Post office boxes, while acceptable for mailing purposes, are unacceptable as a registered office.

3) **The number of directors.** This stipulates the number of directors who are responsible for setting the affairs of the corporation in order.

4) **The initial directors.** List the full names of all of the "founding directors," including middle initials, and generation suffixes. You must also list the complete, legal addresses of all of the directors, including postal codes. These must be the address where service of documents could be delivered to each director. A post office box is not considered a legal address.

5) **The corporate purpose.** The activities of the corporation may be unduly limited unless carefully drawn to be as broad and inclusive as possible. When the powers granted the

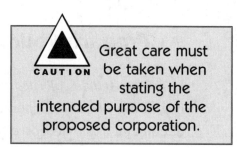

CAUTION Great care must be taken when stating the intended purpose of the proposed corporation.

corporation are not broad enough for its needs, the corporation must petition the granting authority to "amend" its corporate charter by filing *Articles of Amendment* (see later in this chapter) before it may expand its activities beyond those originally approved.

To draft appropriate purposes and activities for the corporation, follow these two steps:

A) Write down a statement setting forth the specific objectives, purposes, and activities the corporation will engage in, including all related lines of business.

B) Add the following statement to allow for future contingencies and protect the right of the corporation to expand future activities:

For example, *The foregoing purposes and activities will be interpreted as examples only and not as limitations, and nothing therein shall be deemed as prohibiting the corporation from extending its activities to any related or otherwise permissible lawful business purposes which may become necessary, profitable or desirable for the furtherance of the corporate objectives expressed above.*

In a construction type business, the corporate purpose might be written as follows:

Purpose: *To engage in the construction, repair and remodeling of buildings and public works of all kinds, and for the improvement of real estate, and the doing of any other business and contracting work incidental to, or connected with such work, including demolition.*

A general merchandising business might write the following corporate purpose:

> ***Purposes:*** *To manufacture, produce, purchase or otherwise acquire, sell, import, export, distribute and deal in goods, wares, services, merchandise and materials of any kind and description.*

The foregoing purposes and activities will be interpreted as examples only and not as limitations, and nothing therein shall be deemed as prohibiting the corporation from engaging in any lawful act or activity for which a corporation may be organized under the *Canada Business Corporations Act.*

6) **Class of shares**. List the classes and number of shares of stock allowed to be sold or distributed. If no maximum number of shares is specified, the corporation will have an unlimited number of each class of shares that the *Articles* provide for.

7) **Rights, privileges, restrictions, and conditions on each class of shares.** If the *Articles* provide for more than one class of shares, the rights of each class must be stated. The right to vote and to receive any remaining property in the event of dissolution must be attached to at least one class of shares.

8) **Restrictions, transfer, and ownership of shares.** List any restrictions or provisions relating to allotment, issue, and transfer, such as the ability to sell the shares outside of the corporation,

9) **Special provisions.** List any special provisions which may be attached to any shares, any restrictions of the corporation, its directors, or its offices.

note If a person is named as a director who was not also named as an incorporator, his or her consent to act as a director must accompany the Articles of Incorporation.

10) **Names of the incorporators.** List the complete names and addresses of all of the incorporators.

The Articles of Incorporation, along with all other appropriate documentation and fees can be processed at Industry Canada's Ottawa office at:

Corporate Directorate
365 Laurier Avenue W.
9th Floor
Ottawa, Ontario K1A 0C8

or at:

Suite 800
5 Ville-Marie
Montreal, Quebec H3B 2G2

or at:

2000 - 300 West George Street
Vancouver, BC V6B 6E1

The Certificate of Incorporation

You are now ready to prepare and file for a *Certificate of Incorporation*. Many provinces will supply you with a blank form or with a model form which must be re-typed. If no specific forms are required, find out what specific information must be included in the Articles of Incorporation.

The following information is typically required:

- name and address of the corporation

- fiscal year

- purposes of the corporation

- total number of shares to be issued (including the par value of shares, and the classes of shares if more than one class)

- preferences, limitations, and rights of each class of stock

> *note* Call the appropriate federal or provincial office where you intend to incorporate to determine whether specific federal or provincial forms are required.

- initial capital paid into the corporation

- number of directors constituting initial board of directors

- name and address of each of the initial directors

- name and address of the president, treasurer and secretary

- name and address of each incorporator

Not all of these items may be required in your province, and many will not apply or be appropriate in your case.

This product is only concerned with business corporations. Professional corporations, non-profit corporations, and corporations in highly regulated industries may require more complicated corporate documents. Anyone entering those fields should seek legal counsel in setting up their business.

Once your Articles of Incorporation have been drafted and signed, they must be mailed or delivered to the appropriate provincial or federal office, depending upon whether you are filing provincially or federally, along with the required fees. You will be notified by return mail that the certificate has been accepted and filed. Your evidence of filing is a receipt from the office.

You may also request a copy of the Articles of Incorporation with the provincial or federal certificate of filing and your official incorporation date. The fee is based on the number of pages in the certificate, and is usually only a few dollars.

At this point the incorporator(s), or person(s) who filed the papers, should hold a meeting, elect the initial board of directors, and turn the management of the corporation over to the board. In many provinces the initial board of directors will be listed in the Articles of Incorporation. The incorporators' meeting, depending upon provincial law, may be an actual meeting, or may be evidenced instead by a signed statement of action.

Certain provinces allow the board (and the stockholders) to transact business without actually meeting—if they all sign a written statement setting forth the action they have taken. Some provinces allow a meeting to take place with the directors communicating by conference telephone call. In this way they can be all over the world and still legally conduct business. Check the law in your province to see if these types of "meetings" or consents are legal.

The initial activity of the board of directors will include:

- electing the officers

- adopting a corporate seal and form of stock certificate

- issuing stock

- opening a corporate bank account

- renting space and similar start-up activities.

Check provincial law to make certain your stock certificate contains all the required information. The stock certificate must show:

- the name of the corporation

- the province of incorporation

- the type of stock (common, preferred, etc.)

- the par value of the share(s)

- any preferences that these or other shares have

- the name of the holder(s)

- signatures of officers of the corporation together with the corporate seal.

> *note* The corporate seal is a simple impression seal which usually contains the name of the corporation, the year of incorporation, and the province of incorporation. It can be purchased at most legal stationery stores and office supply stores at nominal cost.

Articles of Amendment

If you wish to change anything contained in your Articles of Incorporation, e.g., changing from a numbered company to a named company, you must file *Articles of Amendment* with the government that initially granted your *Certificate of Incorporation*. In the case of changing the corporate name, the same rules and regulations apply as if it were an initial incorporation.

Beginning the corporate operation

With your corporation organized, how do you operate and manage it? Here are a few guidelines:

1) Transfer assets to the corporation

If you have been operating a business prior to incorporation (as many people do), you may transfer the assets and debts of the business to the new corporation at an agreed upon sum or consideration, and receive shares of stock in exchange. You cannot, however, burden the corporation with more debts than assets. Further, you cannot sell your personal property to the corporation at inflated prices, nor can you exchange its stock for overvalued personal property.

It is sound business practice to notify all existing business associates, creditors, customers, and clients of the change to corporate status. This can be done by personal communication (telephone or letter), or by a small newspaper notice.

Generally, all subsequent company records and transactions should be changed to reflect the new "corporate" status of the organization, including printing of new letterheads, business cards, stationery, and signage.

2) Choose a fiscal year

You will note that Revenue Canada asks for your *fiscal year*. A fiscal year is any year ending on a date other than December 31. In some provinces, even the Articles of Incorporation require the fiscal year be given. Of course, it is easiest to choose the calendar year as your corporation's fiscal year. However, if that is impossible, a second choice would be July 1 to June 30.

In such a case, for your first year of incorporation, you would have to file two sets of income tax forms: For the first half of the year you would file as a sole proprietor. For the second half of the year, you would file a corporate return—and an individual return—because you are now an employee of your corporation.

Similarly, if you choose April 1, you would file as a sole proprietor for the first quarter (January 1 to March 31), and you would file corporate and individual returns for the last three quarters (April 1 to December 31). If you choose October 1 you would file as a sole proprietor for the first three quarters (January 1 to September 30), and you would file corporate and individual returns for the last quarter (October 1 to December 31).

The advantage of a separate fiscal year is that it allows flexibility in tax planning in the change-over year. And the tax savings, both corporate and personal, could be significant. You may want to choose a fiscal year on the advice of your accountant, who can determine the most advantageous fiscal year for you.

3) Determine provincial and local requirements

Beyond the formalities of incorporation, other regulations and requirements also must be considered. Permits and licenses, for example, are required for such businesses as:

- real estate brokers

- barbers, hairdressers and cosmetologists

- private investigators

- billiard rooms

- health concerns, hospitals ,nursing homes, and pharmacies

- restaurants

- food services

- notaries

- peddlers

- newsstands

- employment agencies

- businesses serving or selling alcoholic beverages

- educational institutions.

Many businesses are regulated by federal agencies, such as:

- brokerage and securities businesses

- air transportation

- banking

- drug manufacturing companies

Before commencing any new business, consider which regulations are applicable so that your business will not be in violation.

In addition, any business that hires employees must consider whether it is subject to:

- withholding taxes for local, provincial, and the federal government

- Canada Pension tax

- unemployment insurance and/or worker's compensation

- whether any unions have jurisdiction and what pension or other payments must be made to them.

Also be aware of minimum wage requirements, the permissibility of hiring minors, and occupational safety and health regulations.

note There are federal and local agencies to assist you in starting your corporation.

A good starting point is your provincial Canadian Business Service Centre (CBSC). In most small business startups, the number of owners of stock is so few that neither the provincial nor federal government need be involved. They will become involved when you are selling stock to a large number of people (usually over 25), or making what is known as a "public offering." However, even with fewer stockholders, there may be some questions about whether your stock sale or your proposed financing must be cleared with the authorities.

Industry Canada provides prospective, new, and established members of the small business community with financial and management training and counselling. Check your yellow pages for their local office.

4) Keep separate corporate records

Remember your corporation is viewed in the eyes of the law as a different "legal entity," separate and apart from its owner(s). Hence, to avoid potential Revenue Canada problems, maintain separate sets of records—one for your personal affairs and one for the affairs of the corporation. As a rule, however, it is not necessary to maintain an elaborate bookkeeping system. Separate bank accounts and bookkeeping clearly show what you and the corporation separately earn and pay out.

> *note*
> A local bookkeeper or accountant can easily set up a convenient accounting and tax system for your business.

5) Apply for a business number

Once your Articles of Incorporation have been filed and approved, you should apply for a *business number*. Even if you already have a business number for a Canada Pension account, or if you have had employees in an unincorporated business, you nevertheless need a new number for the corporation—as the corporation is a "new person" or entity.

6) Set up your corporate bank accounts

To open a corporate bank account, you need a *business number* for your corporation. To obtain a corporate number, simply contact Revenue Canada for the appropriate application. Another item probably required by the bank is a "corporate resolution" to open the bank account, duly signed and embossed with the "corporate seal," as official corporate authorization to open such an account(s).

7) The "extra-provincial" corporation

If your new corporation is a local business, it is unlikely you will need to be authorized or qualified to do business in another province. You clearly are doing business in only one place. But what happens if you start advertising in magazines and you receive orders from other provinces? Are you now doing business in more than one province? What if you have a sales office in one location, but have sales representatives who drive to other provinces and call on potential customers? Does this mean you are now doing business elsewhere? If you start expanding and opening new stores in other provinces, you would clearly be doing business in these other locations.

In all provinces, an unqualified "extra-provincial" is denied access to the courts of the province, which would mean you could not sue someone in that province to enforce a contract or obligation. In addition, many provinces impose fines when it

note If you are doing business in another province but have not qualified by filing the proper papers and paying the fees, the consequences may be serious.

discovers a corporation doing business there without having qualified, and in some cases directors, officers, or agents may also be subject to fines.

The statutes of the provinces define what constitutes "doing business" within that province. While engaging in inter-provincial commerce by itself does not constitute "doing business" within a province, if you engage in such inter-provincial commerce and have a registered office, address, or agent in a province—other than the one in which you are incorporated—you need to register in that province as an extra-provincial corporation. Other principal business activities considered "doing business" are:

- soliciting and receiving orders by mail within that province

- soliciting orders within that province through an agent, sales representative or independent contractor

- shipping orders from a warehouse within that province

- paying provincial taxes

- accepting service of process

Since requirements vary from province to province, you should consult the statutes in any province in which you contemplate one or more of the above activities.

If you find you need authorization to do business as an extra-provincial corporation, the procedure is quite simple. Obtain the application form from that province's appropriate office, complete it, and file it with the proper fees.

Incorporation checklist

Steps in the incorporation process:

1) Decide whether to incorporate.

2) Decide whether to incorporate provincially or federally.

3) Select and apply for a corporate name.

4) Choose a fiscal year.

5) Draft the Articles of Incorporation.

6) Sign the Articles of Incorporation and file with the appropriate filing fees.

7)   Hold the incorporators' initial meeting to elect directors and transact the corporation's first business.

8)   Hold an organizational meeting of the initial board of directors.

9)   Apply for a business number.

10) Select a corporate seal and stock certificates, issue shares, elect officers, and open bank accounts.

11) File a "doing business as" certificate, if necessary.

12) Apply for authorization to do business in other provinces, if necessary.

14) Obtain necessary provincial and local licenses and/or permits.

15) Hold regular, official meetings of directors and stockholders.

16) Document actions and maintain accurate corporate records.

Corporate stock

Corporate stock

A share of stock in a corporation represents a share of the ownership of that corporation. It also represents a proportionate interest in the net value of the company (what would be its value remaining after all of the company's liabilities were satisfied). Each issued share of stock is owned by a shareholder.

When a business incorporates, it issues shares or units of stock indicating who owns what "share" of the incorporated business. These shares are paid for in money, property, or services. Thus, if a corporation's net

note The stockholders of a corporation are the owners of the corporation.

worth is $30,000, and there are 300 shares issued, then, each share would be worth $100. And if there are two shareholders who each own 150 shares of the stock, then each owns half of the corporation.

Types of shares

There are two types of stock—no-par value shares and par value shares:

- **No-Par Value Stock:** No-par value stock bears no stated value on the face of the stock certificate. This type of stock certificate does not represent anything more than the given number of shares or ownership interest in the corporation.

- **Par Value Stock:** Par value stock bears a stated value on the face of the stock certificate (e.g., $10), which represents the amount contributed by the original shareholder(s) to buy each share of stock.

It is generally recommended to incorporate without par value shares. In this manner, you are not restricted to issuing the corporate stock at a restricted value, as you would have to do with par value shares. The price at which you issue par value shares to your incorporators is completely dependent on the amount of equity capital you wish to establish on your corporate books.

The "net worth = value of shares" equation is in no way affected by starting off with par value shares, instead of without par value shares. The equation always remains true. It makes no matter whether you invested $1 for one share or 1¢ for one hundred shares—the value of both types of shares will rise and fall in relation to the net worth of the corporation.

Classes of corporate stock

The two main classes of shares a corporation may issue are *common stock* and *preferred stock*:

- **Common Stock:** Holders of common stock have the primary voice in selecting directors. Voting rights are attached to each share of stock, usually one vote per share. Further, common stockholders are entitled to share in the profits and in final distribution of the corporate assets upon dissolution.

  More than one class of common stock may be issued. Certain conditions may be imposed upon each class, such as voting rights restrictions. They are designated in terms of the rights they may be entitled to, such as Class A-voting stock, Class B-voting stock, etc.

- **Preferred Stock:** The holders of preferred stock usually receive "preference" over the holders of common stock with respect to receipt of dividends and distribution of assets upon dissolution. However, they usually do not have voting rights.

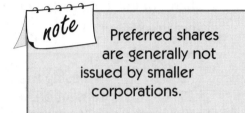

note Preferred shares are generally not issued by smaller corporations.

Both par value and no-par value shares may be issued in different classes. For example, you can have common stock with a par value, or preferred without par value shares, or even cumulative shares, where any dividends or other premiums are accrued—as opposed to being paid on a quarterly basis.

Bear in mind, it's much easier to add rights and/or restrictions at a later date—through a corporate resolution—than attach them at initial issue and have to buy them up or isolate them later. For our purposes, and for the purposes of most small- or medium-sized corporations, only common stock is important. One class of common stock generally serves the needs and purposes of most small corporations, and it is not necessary to authorize or issue a large number of shares of stock. The minimum number of shares allowed under provincial law will be sufficient for most purposes. Beyond this minimum, the provincial government usually imposes a proportionately higher filing fee and tax.

Handling stock certificates

Issuing and cancelling shares

Issuing and cancelling shares of stock is a relatively simple matter of bookkeeping and paperwork. However, you must be careful to differentiate between *initial issues, subsequent issues,* and *transfer of shares between individuals.*

The stock share certificates should be sequentially numbered for ease of accounting for them. Each share certificate may represent any number of shares of the company stock, and each must be hand-signed by at least one of the directors or officers.

> **note**
>
> In closing the transaction, a directors' consent resolution must be prepared and signed by the appropriate director(s) and entered into the Book of Minutes.

Cancelling shares of stock also is comparatively simple. Simply record the cancellation of the share in the record book and write "CANCELLED" across the face of the share certificate. Then staple the cancelled certificate to the stub in the shares certificate book.

Initial issue or allotment

The easiest method for handling initial shares is to have all of the intended shareholders sign the memorandum and indicate the number and kind of shares they subscribed to next to their names. Bear in mind that the first subscribers are automatically named directors of the corporation—until the first meeting of the directors is conducted.

All or some of the original subscribers may choose not to become directors. If such is the case, file a Notice of Directors with your original paperwork. This will release them of responsibility.

In either case, subsequent to the incorporation process prepare a document indicating consent resolutions for election of officers, any asset transfers, and any other transactions which will only require a paragraph or two in the resolutions to document the initial issue of shares.

Stock share issue quantity

Remember, you may set out any number of shares of no-par or par value to be distributed or retained in the treasury. However, there still exist a couple of important issues:

- **Proportion of shares.** During the initial issue, it's not the quantity of shares each shareholder receives rather than the proportion of shares distributed. Just maintain the thought that shareholders are owners, and that their proportion of ownership must remain protected and in perspective.

- **More or less shares**. In certain cases it can be more convenient to issue a larger number shares rather than a smaller number. In this manner, the value of each share would be considerably lower, thereby allowing others to purchase shares at a considerably lower price—bolstering the net worth of the business, while not actually "watering down" the ownership (or voting power) of the original stockholders.

- **Don't issue all the shares**. In the majority of simple corporations, there is no need to distribute all of the shares at the time of incorporation. The unused or unsubscribed for stock is retained in the company treasury and belong to the company until bought, paid for, and delivered.

Post-incorporation issues

Set the price

Sometimes, with the small corporation, another principle stockholder (partner, of sorts) is recruited after the company is running. The question arises as to how much the stock should be valued for the "buy-in."

In a reporting (publicly-held) company, this is insignificant, as the new stockholder just purchases stock at the market price. In the small (non-public) company this becomes more difficult. However, par value shares may not be issued at below their par value. If the shares are non-par value, the directors have the authority to set the price at their discretion.

Tax considerations

In setting the prices of new issues, the Income Tax Act provides that new issues priced below their fair market value would carry a capital gains tax for the difference between the price paid and the fair market value of the shares issued.

In the case of employees, they are allowed to buy additional shares of the company—at any price—without having received any tax benefit. The only stipulation here is that the employee must keep the shares in his or her name for a period of two years. Should the employee choose to redeem or sell the stock after that date, the employee would then realize a capital gain or loss.

Pro-rata basis

The existing shareholders have *pre-emptive rights* to prevent the possibility of a company issuing new shares in an effort to water down the rights of the minority shareholders.

> **note** The practical effect of the pro-rata basis allows each shareholder to maintain his or her position of ownership in relation to the other stockholders.

In order to allow shareholders these pre-emptive rights, the directors must offer a pro-rata share (on a proportional basis to the existing stockholders' share of ownership) purchase to the existing shareholders prior to setting new and lower prices.

Consent of existing shareholders

After a subscription for an allotment of a specific number of shares, existing shareholders must sign a consent and waiver before the corporate resolutions may be written to allow this new allotment.

Should the current stockholders reject this consent and waiver, then the directors must solicit each of the shareholders individually, within a specific time frame. Should no acceptances or declinations be received, the directors are free to authorize the new allotment. However, the new allotment may not be sold in a more favorable light than those already possessed by the current shareholders.

Transfer of shares

This refers to the simple transfer of shares from one shareholder to another.

Transfers of stock are regulated by the company's Articles. Basically speaking, the existing shareholders have the first right of refusal to acquire the shares or block of stock being offered. Should the existing stockholders decline to purchase the full number of the offered shares, the offering shareholder may:

- Decline to sell the shares not accepted.

- Offer the remaining shares pro-rata to the shareholders who first accepted the offer.

- Sell the remaining shares to third parties, who may not even be present shareholders. However, he or she cannot sell the shares on more favorable terms than offered to the existing shareholders.

Share redemption

Your corporation is allowed to buy back shares of stock from shareholders that have a right of redemption attached to the shares. The corporation can purchase these redemption shares:

- only if such purchase or redemption will not place the company into an insolvent financial position

- it must offer to purchase the shares on a pro-rata basis, the same way it must issue on a pro-rata (in proportion to the percentage of stock ownership) basis (if a non-reporting company)

In some cases, the shares may contain a *stock redemption agreement*, which provides that the corporation will purchase back the departing shareholder's interests upon the occurrence of a triggering event, such as the acquisition of a specified asset.

Under the stock redemption agreement, the shareholders enter into a binding contract with the corporation for the purchase of the shareholders' interests. This agreement obligates the shareholders (or their estates) to sell, and the corporation to buy the shares of the departing shareholder at an agreed-upon or determinable price. Under a redemption agreement, *only* the corporation is obligated to purchase the shares.

Management of the corporation

Management of the corporation **5**

Bylaws are drawn up and adopted at the first meeting of the stockholders. Subject to any restrictions imposed by the corporate charter or bylaws, the right and responsibility to determine policy and conduct the business of the corporation lies with the *board of directors*. The number of those who make up the board is usually set by the bylaws of the corporation.

Corporate directors

The directors are elected by the stockholders and are ultimately responsible to the stockholders. Stockholders have the power to remove directors, either for cause or without cause, when the charter of incorporation or the bylaws so authorize, and at any special meeting of the stockholders called for that purpose. Directors are usually elected annually at the annual meeting of stockholders.

It is important to remember that stockholders actually vote their shares of stock. Thus, if there are three stockholders but one owns 80% of the shares of stock, that stockholder will control the vote based on the amount of stock ownership.

There is a difference between a corporation's charter and its bylaws. If any restrictions imposed on the general powers of the directors are contained in the corporation's charter, third parties are bound by them, since the charter is considered a public record. Restrictions embodied only in the corporate bylaws, however, are not binding upon third persons, as bylaws are not publicly filed or recorded.

The following rules govern directors:

- Directors must act as a body.

- Directors can bind the corporation only by actions taken at a board meeting with the necessary quorum.

- Directors cannot vote by proxy and their duties generally may not be delegated to others.

- A resolution not passed at a board meeting but signed by each individual director at his home would be invalid, unless the directors happened to be the sole stockholders.

The directors are generally required by law to meet at least once every year, although as a practical matter this is rarely done in family or small corporations. In such meetings, the directors appoint the corporate officers (however, the same officers are often re-elected), ratify acts of the prior year, review important business matters and set broad policy objectives. The corporate secretary then writes up "minutes" as a record of the meetings. The directors may also authorize dividends, a new contract, a new lease, a loan, major purchases or projects. Such actions are then recorded in the form of *corporate resolutions* and are formally recorded in the *minutes book* of the corporation.

As a practical matter, minutes of director's and stockholder's meetings are often very helpful as an instrument of management, since they are frequently the only official records of what was done or decided upon by these bodies.

> **note** When accurately and adequately kept, the minutes will sometimes help avoid misunderstandings and potential lawsuits.

Provided the board of directors acts honestly, the directors may generally bind the corporation by actions taken at board meetings and are not personally liable for any such actions. Therefore, if bad or imprudent judgment should result in business losses, the directors may not be held personally liable, unless the action was grossly negligent or made in bad faith.

Directors may be personally liable if they:

- Exploit their office for personal gain at the expense of the corporation or its stockholders. The directors are usually said to have a "fiduciary," or special, relationship with the stockholders that presumes utmost good faith and trust.

- Wrongfully dispose of corporate assets.

- Declare and pay dividends when no surplus or profit exists.

- Authorize the issue of unissued stock to themselves for the purpose of converting themselves from minority to majority stockholders.

- Issue, as fully paid, shares of stock not fully paid for.

- Improperly lend corporate funds to stockholders when such funds remain unpaid or uncollectible.

Eight liability traps for directors

Corporate directorships are increasingly hazardous and are a surefire way to attract liability. Directors incur civil and criminal liability in many ways other than through their negligent management. However, eight lesser known but chronic trouble spots worth noting include:

1) **Improper dividends:** Dividends that are unlawfully declared make the directors personally liable to the creditors for any resulting corporate insolvency. Delaware alone permits dividends from funds other than earned surplus.

2) **Shareholder loans:** Directors who allow the corporation to make loans to an officer or stockholder may be liable if the borrower fails to repay. Directors must prudently authorize insider loans.

3) **Unpaid taxes**: Corporate officers are usually the responsible parties for unpaid U.S. withholding taxes. Certain states also impose automatic liability on directors for unpaid state taxes. Directors can become liable for unpaid federal withholding taxes if the IRS can prove that the directors controlled corporate funds and determined whether the withholding taxes were paid.

4) **Improper payments upon dissolution:** Directors also become liable to creditors when they authorize dissolution of the corporation and distributions of proceeds to stockholders before creditors are fully paid.

5) **Securities violations:** Directors seldom realize their liability to investors for false and misleading statements in the corporation's prospectus. Outsider or unaffiliated directors must particularly verify the accuracy of a registration because the SEC imposes this special burden upon outside directors. Directors who resign before the registration is filed cannot become liable.

6) **Anti-trust violations:** Directors may be personally liable for anti-trust violations that they reasonably should have been aware of as corporate directors. Liability in these cases can be particularly costly because any recovery against the directors can be triple the actual damages.

7) **Civil rights and discrimination violations:** This is a comparatively new source of liability for corporate directors and arises when directors approve or allow corporate policies that violate these laws.

8) **Environmental law violation:** Another rapidly expanding problem for directors of companies is the potential for hazardous waste violations, particularly when the directors actually have knowledge of hazardous waste conditions and take no action to prevent further waste.

Corporate officers

The president, vice president, treasurer, and secretary (and such other officers as a particular corporation may choose to have) are appointed by the board of directors. The officers' salaries, duties, and conditions of employment are fixed by the board.

The officers run and manage the corporation from day to day. However, they have only such legitimate responsibilities and authority to act on behalf of the board of directors as are conferred upon them by the board, or as are specified in the bylaws of the corporation.

note Corporations are required to have a president, treasurer, and secretary (or clerk). Other officers, such as chairperson, vice president, or assistant treasurer, are optional and are not usually included in the Articles of Incorporation.

Corporate records

Corporate records

A corporation has shareholders, directors and officers. The shareholders are the owners of the corporation, and determine who become directors of the corporation. These directors are responsible for the overall management of the corporation and, in turn, appoint officers such as the president, vice-president, secretary, and treasurer.

Minute book and seal

Corporations must keep written records of events such as annual shareholders' meetings, and confirm the occurrence of such meetings with the government. These result in *Corporate By-Laws*, as well as *Director* and *Shareholder Resolutions*, which define many aspects of a corporation. Appropriate records must also be maintained of directors and shareholders, even if there is only one of each.

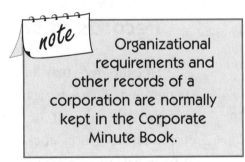

note Organizational requirements and other records of a corporation are normally kept in the Corporate Minute Book.

The corporate minutes book is important for many reasons:

- Parties dealing with the corporation may want evidence that the corporate action was approved.

- Officers and employees within the corporation are entitled to protection if their acts were approved.

- Accurate minutes are frequently necessary to preserve certain tax benefits or to avoid tax liabilities and penalties.

- Minutes are often necessary to prove that the corporation is operated as a separate entity independent of its principals.

Generally, you need only complete the resolution that conforms to the corporate action voted. Occasionally, however, you may need to modify the form to suit your particular needs. Always be certain the resolution accurately states the corporate action approved. In some cases, particularly with the more important transactions, you may find it necessary to have a lawyer decide what the resolution should contain. While these prepared forms can greatly simplify your recordkeeping requirements, they are not a substitute for your good judgment in deciding how you should document the actions of your corporation.

note A corporate seal is used to emboss the corporation's name on legal documents. Typically, the first application of a corporate seal is the opening of a corporate bank account.

Records of stockholder actions

Stockholders may usually vote on the broadest issues relating to the corporation. These typically include change of corporate name, address, or purpose, the amount or type of shares, and other matters involving the corporate structure. Stockholders' action may also be needed for major legal or financial issues, such as whether to mortgage, encumber, pledge or lease all or substantially all of the corporate assets or to file bankruptcy, merge or consolidate. There are, of course, many other actions that can be taken by stockholders. The primary function of the stockholders, however, is to elect the board of directors, through whose governance the corporation is actually managed.

Stockholders may only act officially as a group. This means that a formal meeting is needed before they can legally bind the corporation. There are some exceptions, when the stockholders can consent in writing to a particular action without having to hold a meeting. These instances, however, are rare.

Certain rules and procedures have to be followed for stockholders to conduct an official stockholder meeting:

1) Every stockholder has to be properly notified about the time and place of the meeting, who is calling the meeting, and any matters that will be considered at the meeting. It is common in small corporations for the stockholders to do without a formal notice of time and place of meeting, especially where the bylaws set the time and place of the annual meeting of stockholders. This can be done by having all the stockholders sign a waiver of notice at the meeting. Unscheduled or special meetings of stockholders may require notice, although a signed waiver of notice can also be used at these meetings. For an unscheduled meeting to be legally convened, it is essential that the records show that proper notice was given, or that the stockholders signed a waiver of notice.

Your Certificate of Incorporation or bylaws will specify where and when a stockholder meeting can legally be held and the book of minutes should show the time and place of each meeting. In this way, you can prove that the meeting complied with the legal requirements.

2) No business may be transacted at a stockholders' meeting unless the required number of members (as listed in the bylaws) is present. Therefore, it is essential that the book of minutes reflects the quorum of stockholders who attended the meeting. The Certificate of Incorporation or the bylaws will usually state the size of the quorum, either in terms of the number of stockholders or the number of shares that must be represented at the meeting. For example, a bylaw that "two-thirds of all stockholders shall constitute a quorum" applies to the number of stockholders, and not to the

amount of the stock they own. On the other hand, a bylaw that states "a majority of the outstanding stock shall constitute a quorum" means that a certain number of shares of stock

note

If no bylaw addresses a quorum, then whatever number of stockholders shows up for the meeting will constitute a quorum.

must be represented, regardless of whether the stock is owned by one person or by thousands of people.

3) Stockholder meetings must have a chairperson to preside over the meeting. They must also have a secretary to record what happened. The bylaws will ordinarily designate these officials by specifying that the president serve as chairperson and the secretary act as secretary. However, substitutes are usually allowable.

4) The first item of business at every stockholder meeting should be to approve the minutes of the previous meeting. Once the minutes are approved, they legally document what occurred at the meeting. Minutes are the most conclusive proof of what the corporation is authorized to do. That is why it is important to show that the minutes have been approved as accurate, or that necessary changes have been made.

5) Parliamentary procedure governs the conduct of meetings. It is not generally necessary to identify the person making the motion or seconding a motion. Nor is it essential to record the exact tally of votes, as long as the action approved is clear.

Records of director actions

Most of the rules and procedures that apply to stockholder meetings apply equally to meetings of the board of directors, with these exceptions:

- Directors will meet more often than stockholders, and in large corporations may meet monthly. The directors can also hold special meetings for interim board action. In more active corporations they will routinely meet more often.

- The board, as with stockholders, can only function through a duly called meeting where a quorum of directors (as defined in the bylaws) is present. Directors who may be in conflict with the interests of the corporation may, however, not be counted toward the quorum or not be entitled to vote.

- The board must be particularly careful to document its actions and why the action was taken. Because the board has responsibility to stockholders—and potential liability to other constituencies—it may be called upon to show why its action was prudent, particularly in areas of dividends, loans to officers, major contracts, compensation, and policy-making. It is especially critical for the minutes to include or refer to reports, arguments, opinions, and other documents to support the reasonableness of the board's actions.

- Frequently the board will be called upon to issue "certified resolutions" or "certificates of vote," which conclusively show to third parties dealing with the corporation that the person acting on behalf of the corporation has the required authority.

All records, resolutions and minutes should be kept within the corporate minute book for no fewer than six years—although retaining the records for longer is recommended, considering the numerous types of claims that are possible and the varying statutes of limitation.

Funding your

corporation

Funding your corporation

Funds may come from many different sources, but no matter what the source, capital originates from two broad categories: internal and external.

- **Internal sources include your own assets.** You are essentially financing part or all of the business yourself—either with cash or a loan. Cash, investments, real estate, other businesses that you own, or anything else that can be converted to cash or used as collateral for a loan qualifies as capital.

- **External sources include capital from sources other than yourself.** You may borrow money from a relative, a bank, a finance company, mortgage company or even use a credit card.

> *note*
> It is often necessary to provide some internal capital in order to qualify for external capital.

Most lenders are reluctant to provide all the money you need for a new, as yet unproven business. So the best way to express your commitment and confidence and to maintain some control is to use at least some of your own money. This is also known as "blood money" or "blood equity." Lenders are doubly impressed if you were especially creative, innovative, or resourceful in finding this money.

Shrewdly finance your corporation

Funds that you loan to your own corporation are funds that you can easily lose. You can reduce or eliminate this risk of loss by correctly structuring your loan to your corporation.

The wrong way to finance your corporation is to directly invest in your corporation, whether it is for shares (equity) or as a loan. If your business fails, you will be only another unsecured creditor and reclaim none or little of your original investment.

The shrewd owner secures him/herself with the business' assets. Their claim then becomes superior to general creditor claims. Strategy: Have your bank directly loan your business the necessary funds with your business pledging its assets to the bank as collateral. Your bank will lend to the business since you can pledge personal assets as collateral for the loan. The 100 percent secured loan thus provides the bank no risk. Should your business fail, your bank will be its secured party and the first creditor to be repaid from liquidating the business's assets. And once repaid, your bank would relinquish the personal assets you pledged as security.

note Always safeguard your investment. Use your bank as your helpful intermediary to insure your investment will be recouped should your business fail.

But do take this strategy one step further. You may have a friend or relative guarantee your bank loan, while you pledge your collateral to this intermediary who then pledges it to the bank. Since you are not the bank's direct guarantor, a business failure would not jeopardize the bank's secured claim against the business' assets. And with the bank repaid, your collateral would revert back to you through your intermediary.

Before investing or loaning money to your corporation, review this with your lawyer. It is not too complicated an arrangement, and your lawyer and bank can easily structure the deal—you then have two big advantages. First, funds you invest in your business are now more fully protected than if you had invested the funds for stock or made an unsecured loan. Second, you now indirectly control the mortgage on your business and can also indirectly protect your business from other creditors.

Sources of funding

External funding sources may be further divided into two categories:

Formal—The most common formal source of funds is the private venture capitalist. Private venture capitalists finance start-up and early stage businesses in exchange for an equity interest in the business itself. They are professional investors who usually insist upon having a strong management role in your company. And, if you are successful, they may ultimately seek ownership control.

A second popular formal source of funds is "incubators." These are organizations sponsored by associations, often colleges and universities, with their own pool of money to lend. They also can be valuable in putting you in touch with other lending organizations.

Informal—"Angels" provide 85% of all funding for start-up businesses. An "angel" is an informal investor who:

- provides initial capital for new businesses

- offers fair repayment terms

- does not seek to control or take advantage of the business owner

An "angel" could be your doctor, attorney, employer, supplier, customer, stockbroker, friend, or relative—anyone who has money to invest or who knows of someone with money to invest. Simply look in the "Business

Opportunities" section of newspapers and magazines. There are many classified ads for "Capital to Invest," "Money to Lend," or some other variation. There will be conditions, requirements, and specific terms, but every one of these ads leads to money potentially available to your business.

Most "angels" prefer not to be the sole investor, so they can put you in touch with other investors. Your chance of convincing an "angel" to invest is one out of five—a much higher percentage than with that of venture capitalists.

Ask for money indirectly

Never directly approach your potential investor and ask for money. Use the three-step indirect approach:

1) describe your idea in detail

2) explain that you are uncomfortable asking him for money for fear it might strain the relationship

3) ask your potential investor to pass your business plan and request for money on to someone who he thinks would be interested.

If your potential investor is intrigued by your idea, he will begin reading the business plan himself and begin negotiations with you shortly thereafter. If he is not able to invest at this time, he will probably pass your request on to someone who is in a position to do so.

Once you have secured some investment capital, it becomes much easier to raise the rest. Many investors feel more comfortable knowing that others have "taken the plunge" before them, while others will agree to invest provided you have a firm commitment from others to raise the balance needed.

What makes a good investor?

The more of the following traits your investor has, the more successful your relationship with him will be. A good investor is:

1) able to provide additional funding as the growth of the business warrants

2) willing to provide physical or managerial help in emergencies

3) experienced with successful start-up businesses.

4) comfortable with the risks inherent in a new businesses

5) fair as far as the terms of repayment.

6) reasonable to the extent of day-to-day participation

7) agreeable to leaving the company

8) willing to sign a confidentiality agreement. This protects you from having an investor become your competition.

Six deal-breakers you must avoid

A well-prepared business plan must provide lenders the answers they need before they will agree to invest. The following are the six most frequent reasons deals never happen:

1) **The business plan is written from the wrong perspective—** from that of the borrower. Instead, it must be written with the lender in mind. It must address his questions, his needs, and his fears. It must describe how the lender will benefit—not the borrower.

2) **The anticipated growth rate is too low.** There must be sufficient growth potential to justify the initial investment. You must find out the reasonable growth rate for your business. Will your anticipated growth rate be higher or lower than the industry standard?

note The business plan must address the investor's lack of knowledge by providing sufficient detail to address the uninformed investor's questions.

3) **The lender is not familiar with the industry.** This leads to lack of confidence in the investment.

4) **The borrower and his management team lack the day-to-day talent and experience to run the company.** Proving you have hired or can hire the right employees is critical to your success.

5) **Lack of personal equity in the business.** You have not invested any of your own money in the business, why should someone else? This is viewed as a lack of personal commitment and faith in the business.

6) **Inability to meet or beat the competition.** You do not own anything unique—a product, technology, territory, service, patent, copyright, brand, or marketing plan.

Credit card financing

Small companies often use credit card debt as a short-term source of funds. However, it must never replace traditional methods of financing because of the extremely high debt the business will incur. Beyond short term, such high interest rates can seriously strain any business.

This type of financing is most often used to fund a start-up business. By using multiple high-limit credit cards and planning well in advance, a business can often raise 25 thousand, 50 thousand, even 100 thousand dollars all of which must be repaid with interest. Therefore, it is critical that the business have a profit margin high enough to offset the high interest.

Bank
financing

Bank financing

8

You probably already deal with a bank, even if it is only a savings and checking account. But borrowing money to fund a business is much more complex than obtaining a home mortgage, a car loan, or passbook savings loan. To obtain a business loan you must first forget four common myths:

> **HOT spot** Banks are the most obvious source of external financing when you want to borrow money for a business.

Myth #1: Banks are in business to lend money. False! Banks do not lend money, bankers do. Bankers are in business to make money. Money is their inventory and they use it to make profitable loans.

Myth #2: Bankers have standard loan policies. This is also false. There is no "standard" loan policy. All loans are negotiable.

Myth #3: Bankers have unlimited loan funds. Again, this is false. Bankers have limited money to lend, and you must compete for those dollars. Therefore, they lend money chiefly on the basis of security and safety in what is a highly competitive process.

Myth #4: Bankers do not need your business. Fortunately, this is also false. Yes, you need a bank's money, but the bank equally needs your business.

Establishing the banking relationship

Everything revolves around the banker. Therefore, the key to negotiating the perfect loan is to establish a strong positive relationship with your banker before you apply for funding. A banker is a person. It is much easier to say "no" to a stranger than to a friend.

- Do you know your banker's lending limit, his boss' lending limit, or the bank's lending limit?

- Have you recently introduced another customer to the bank?

- Do you socialize with your banker or his boss?

- Do you know your banker's interests or hobbies?

- Does your attorney or accountant know your banker?

Ask friends, business associates, lawyers, and accountants to refer you to a particular banker. They are likely to refer you to someone they have had a positive experience with. You will also be able to mention that person's name when you call for an appointment.

Setting the appointment

When you call for an appointment, you will first speak to the banker's secretary. It is she who sets his appointments, screens his calls, and generally organizes his banking life. Therefore, get to know the secretary. Be friendly and polite. Mention the name of the person referring you.

The interview

Bankers have highly structured schedules. Tell the banker that you will not take up much of his time and that you will leave your business plan with him—to read at his convenience. Explain that you are interviewing several local bankers not just to borrow money, but also to find the bank that can service your company's needs for years to come. Ask direct questions about the bank's experience lending to your type of business, industry, or with your product.

HINT

Think of your meeting with the banker as an interview in which you interview each other.

Ask him about the bank's resources in the following areas:

- **Assets**—What is the rate of growth of the bank's asset base?

- **Large exposure limits**—Does the bank conduct a large part of its business with a single client?

- **Management**—Who is on the board of directors? How long has the daily management team been in place?

- **Earnings**—Has the bank's quarterly and annual earnings kept pace with the financial sector?

- **Liquidity**—Does the bank maintain sufficient cash and assets to meet its obligations?

- **Loss provisions**—Since it is unlikely that any financial institution will receive all of the money owed it, does the bank currently maintain provisions to recognize these losses?

- **Systems and controls**—Does the bank operate efficiently? Does it update its policies and procedures to minimize risk?

Each category receives a separate rating from 1 to 5 with 1 being the highest and 5 the lowest rating. A composite score is then calculated to give the bank an overall rating. This is public information.

The loan committee

Every banker who is a loan officer has the ability to lend up to a specified limit without facing the loan committee. The loan committee is made up of other loan officers and members of the bank who unfortunately do not know you. They will accept or reject your loan request based solely upon the three Cs of loansmanship:

1) **Character**—Does your credit history justify the loan?

2) **Cash Flow**—Does the business provide sufficient cash flow and profit to repay the loan?

3) **Collateral**—How much risk will the bank have if you fail to repay the loan? Will the bank have the collateral to recover the loan?

Ask your banker whether your loan would have to go before the loan committee. If the loan is granted, would all subsequent requests have to do so? Find out as much as you can about your banker's independent lending limit.

Find out what additional information besides your business plan you will need to supply. This may include:

- tax returns

- income projections

- bios of key personnel

- employment history

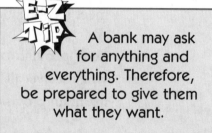

A bank may ask for anything and everything. Therefore, be prepared to give them what they want.

- letters of reference

- marketing plan

Seven tips to negotiate your perfect loan

Aggressively negotiate favorable loan terms. Follow these six rules, and you will save big money on your loan:

1) **Negotiate interest.** Interest rates are always negotiable. If the bank agrees that your business plan is sound, it can drop interest rates several points. This can save you many thousands of dollars.

2) **Demand the longest possible loan period.** This conserves cash by lowering your monthly payments.

3) **Pledge only business assets as collateral.** This protects your personal assets in the event of a loan default. Even if you have signed a personal guarantee and the business defaults, the proceeds from the auction may be sufficient to satisfy the bank.

4) **Never falsify the loan application.** Falsifying information can result in immediate foreclosure, prevent you from discharging your debt in bankruptcy, and even bring criminal charges.

5) **Never borrow personally.** Your corporation must borrow the money, not you. If you personally borrow the money, then the bank cannot claim the business assets if you default. You will have to repay the loan personally. Obtain the help of an attorney with this.

6) **Never settle for the first offer.** There are plenty of banks. Shop for the best deal at at least four banks and compare.

7) **Agree to do your corporate banking with the bank supplying the funds.** However, in the event you personally guaranteed the loan, be careful about doing your personal banking with the same bank. In the event of default, the bank will have access to your money.

Types of loans

There are four basic types of commercial loans:

1) **Single-payment loan**—This is a short-term loan usually for one year or less. It is targeted for a specific purpose.

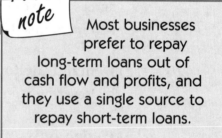

note Most businesses prefer to repay long-term loans out of cash flow and profits, and they use a single source to repay short-term loans.

2) **Installment loan**—This may be a short- or long-term loan with fixed monthly payments.

3) **Term loan**—This is long-term loan with fixed monthly or quarterly payments.

4) **Revolving line of credit**—This is a type of fixed amount loan from which the business may draw upon when needed and replace when convenient. Interest continues to accrue on outstanding balance.

What do bankers look for?

There are five elements every banker examines when evaluating a loan request:

1) **The amount of the loan**. Is the amount realistic?

2) **The purpose of the loan.** What is the money specifically going to be used for?

3) **When will the loan be repaid?** Is this a long- or short-term loan?

4) **What if the loan cannot be repaid when due?** What plans do you have or steps will you take to meet this contingency?

Additionally, there are five more key areas of concern:

1) **Management of the business.** Is the management experienced? Will it meet the challenges of a small business head on or hope the problem goes away?

2) **Accounting and bookkeeping system.** Does it provide adequate and accurate information using generally accepted accounting principles?

3) **Is there a dynamic market for the product or service?** Can you supply the banker with independent research showing industry growth projections for the next five years?

4) **Business structure.** Will the business take advantage of outside expertise? Does it plan to outsource or use consultants?

Is the company likely to be profitable? Here, realistic cash flow projections and pro-forma profit and loss projections are extremely valuable in accessing the likelihood of future profitability. Can the banker reasonably rely upon those projections?

What if your loan application is denied?

You basically have two choices—try another bank or keep trying at the same bank. Sometimes it just takes the next person up the ladder to get a loan approved. First, find out from the denying loan officer why the loan was rejected. Be sure to get a detailed answer—not just a cursory comment. Next,

> **HOT spot** Remember, all loan decisions are subjective. Never be embarrassed or angry.

ask what you would have to do to get the loan approved. Some loan officers always look at an application with an eye towards turning it down, while others try to find reasons to accept it. If you get no help here, follow the chain of command all the way up to the board of directors, if necessary. Often your persistence and determination will tip the scales in your favor.

Alternative funding sources

9

Alternative funding sources

It is considerably easier to finance an existing business than a startup because an existing business has both a track record and assets, and most business lenders are asset-based.

The following assets are valuable collateral:

- Receivables
- Inventory

- Contracts
- Leases

- Cash flow
- Trademark and patent rights

- Fixtures and equipment
- Customer lists

- Money in the bank
- Real estate

Where the money is

Besides banks, there are many financing sources for your business:

- Time sharing
- Sellers

- Leases
- Suppliers

- Accounts receivable
- Motor vehicles
- Inventory
- Sale-leaseback

- Brokers
- Life insurance
- Partners/investors
- Franchising

Each financing source is only one part of the overall financing puzzle and they are often used in combination to create 100 percent financing. Master these money sources. They can be your keys to opportunity.

How to borrow your down payment

Borrowing your down payment for an existing business requires a different strategy than arranging a long term loan with a hefty down payment. Bankers want you to use your own money to match theirs whether you start or buy a business. Conversely, your down payment loan will be short term (usually for one year or less) and typically for about 20 percent of the purchase price. You cannot pledge the

> **HOT** spot The secret is never to reveal to the bank that you need the loan for a down payment on the business.

business assets to the bank as collateral because they will probably be pledged to a lender who financed the lion's share of the price. Try these perfectly legal techniques to raise your down payment.

- **Borrow multiple loans simultaneously.** This strategy legally increases your borrowing power five- to ten-fold. Even with limited personal assets, if you can obtain a small, unsecured loan, perhaps $2,000, only on your signature, then five banks should collectively loan you $10,000. Of course, once you receive the first loan, you must disclose it on later credit applications. However, if you simultaneously apply for loans at five banks, you can truthfully state that you have no other outstanding loans. This effectively increases your borrowing power. This technique won't work if the application asks about "loans applied for." Fortunately, few ask this question.

- **Tap the power of pyramid loans.** The pyramid strategy involves two banks and some beginning capital–say $3,000. Here too, you will borrow $3,000 on your signature alone following these easy steps: First, apply for a $3,000 loan payable in 30 days at a local bank. Then place these loan proceeds in a high-interest bearing account at another bank. In 25 days withdraw the $3,000 and pay your first bank. About two weeks later return to the first bank and apply for a $6,000 loan. You'll probably receive it because you now have good credit. Invest the $6,000 and again repay the loan in 25 days. Finally, in the third month repeat the entire process with a $10,000 loan. Pay it ahead of schedule, and the bank will gladly lend you $15,000. Each loan fortifies your credit rating and your borrowing power. Soon you have your down payment.

- **Find a co-signer, perhaps a friend or relative.** This request is often easier for them to grant than asking them to actually make the loan.

Once you have your down payment, loan it to your business. You then quickly repay yourself and pay the bank. You will have eliminated your investment risk, released whatever collateral you pledged, and improved your credit rating. Most importantly, you will have completed a no-cash-down deal.

Structure the package for total financing

You can even borrow 100 percent of the purchase price of a business from a bank. How is this possible when banks usually lend only 50-60 percent of the purchase price? Consider that a small business is difficult to accurately appraise. You can, therefore, often increase the purchase price of the business in order to obtain a higher loan. How can this be legal? You might increase the purchase price on the contract and decrease the consideration on the non-compete agreement. Suppose the seller wants $50,000 for the business and $50,000 for an agreement not to compete with you. The bank may only be willing to lend you $25,000 or 50 percent of the selling price of the business itself. If you increase the selling price to $100,000 and reduce the non-compete agreement to $1.00, you will wind up with $50,000 for the business on a 50 percent loan. $50,000 is exactly the amount of money you need. This does not suggest that you should ever deliberately mislead a lender, and you certainly should have an attorney guide you to avoid legal problems.

Why seller financing may be your best bet

Seller financing is often the best money source for buying a business. Many financial experts will advise you to ignore other sources until the seller has given you his final "no." This is because seller financing features five big advantages:

1) **Sellers are less "interest-hungry."** Sellers do not finance to earn interest. They finance to sell their business. A smart seller realizes that this may be the only way to make a deal. A highly motivated seller may even finance you with dramatically lower interest payments. You are still likely to pay a higher rate than the seller could receive on his money from a bank, so the seller will still earn a profit on his loan. However, the seller chiefly wants to sell his business.

HOT spot Remember, every point you save in interest puts money in your pocket.

2) **Sellers will wait longer for their money**. Banks typically want their money in five years. But the longer the loan period, the smaller the payments. This obviously puts less strain on your cash flow and lets your business grow faster. Not even friends or relatives are likely to agree to long payouts, but sellers often extend notes for seven to ten years. Even 15 to 20 year rates are common. For these sellers financing creates an annuity.

3) **Sellers will finance more of the price.** Sellers know what their business is worth because they have their money tied up in it. They don't have to be as cautious as banks because if you do default the seller can easily step in and take back the business. The seller can more easily resell the business, while a bank or other lender must liquidate the business. So sellers can afford to be more lenient about how much of the price they will finance. Your goal should be 70-100 percent seller financing.

4) **Sellers will not demand outside personal collateral. Why?** The seller has the best collateral in the world—his own business. Sellers seldom have the courage to demand additional collateral. You may have to offer personal guarantees, and the seller will require a mortgage on the business, but you have a powerful argument for refusing personal collateral. "If the business isn't adequate collateral for your $50,000 loan, it's not worth the $65,000 I'm paying you for it." It's a persuasive argument.

5) **Sellers can be more forgiving.** Sellers understand the nature of their own business. If business is slow, and you miss a payment or two, a seller is apt to be more forgiving than will banks where the entire chain of command panics over a "problem loan." Perhaps, the seller was once in the same embarrassing position.

> **HINT** A seller has no one breathing down his neck, and he is not as likely to foreclose impatiently.

Sellers understand cash flow problems, and you can usually reason with them. And now that the business is finally sold, do you think the seller really wants it back?

Let suppliers finance your business

Your suppliers may make as much, or even more money from your business as you. Since they too will benefit from your business, why not have them contribute to your venture? Once they see their profit potential from your business, they may eagerly advance you your down payment. Supplier financing works well with any business that purchases inventory. Key suppliers are the logical financing sources because they will reap the biggest rewards from your business. Suppliers have small risk from financing if they are adequately secured with business assets. Don't be shy. If you succeed you will sell their products and earn them many times their investment for years to come.

How do you get a supplier loan? First, convince the supplier that it will be mutually beneficial. Focus on the business' primary suppliers. Businesses purchase most of their inventory from only a few suppliers. Secondary or "fill in" suppliers are poor loan candidates. Target primary suppliers that are themselves family-owned businesses. They have more flexibility to make customer loans than do large, national firms.

Estimate the annual business you can give the supplier. What is the supplier's gross profit on that merchandise? Now negotiate. Your deal is for your supplier to lend you money in exchange for your profitable business. Don't be afraid to ask for a loan that equals about six month's worth of projected profits to the supplier. The more competitive your industry, the more you may request. Of course, your supplier will want to be paid quickly, and will never accept a loan unless it can be safely repaid from future cash flow. Your supplier also will be greatly concerned about the safety of his loan, so offer a mortgage on the businesses assets and, if necessary, your personal guarantee. Your supplier also will expect your agreement to purchase a minimum amount of merchandise over a specified time. Failure to comply may cause a loan default.

Let your supplier see you in the best possible light. Let him visualize how he will benefit from your growing business. Let him know you will feature his most profitable lines. Detail your expansion plans. Highlight his prior profitable relationship with the business. Recruit a few of the supplier's major customers to endorse you. The supplier may accommodate you to please them. Existing suppliers lend for fear of losing a good account. Prospective suppliers lend to win new business. In either case, the supplier who foresees that the loan will yield exceptional dividends is a supplier ready to open his checkbook.

Remember, buying power is borrowing power.

Turn the broker's commission into your down payment

Business brokers handle about two out of three businesses sold so you have a solid opportunity to have your broker help you with your financing. How? Recruit your broker as your partner in the down payment. Consider that a 20 percent down payment is about average on any deal. Brokers receive 10 percent of the selling price as their commission. The commission then amounts to about half the down payment. Convince the broker that you can finance most of the purchase price but cannot raise the entire down payment. The broker may then agree to loan you part of his commission rather than lose the sale and all of his commission. However, play fair with the broker. Quickly repay the loan. Pay interest, and secure the loan with collateral.

Use the broker's commission gambit when there is no broker. How? Simply ask the seller to reduce the price (and the down payment) by showing the seller how much less he may have pocketed had a broker been involved. This is a powerful negotiating tactic.

Customers will bankroll you

Customer financing works beautifully with certain businesses. Does your target business offer a unique product or service? Does it serve a particular market or group of customers? If so, your customers may pay you in advance for what you can offer them. For example, advance subscriptions to a new magazine may give a publisher the capital to print and mail the first several issues. Or a medical company with a new animal vaccine may borrow its start up costs against advance orders from thousands of veterinarians. A Chinese restaurant may rent its largest dining room to bridge clubs during the day. There are thousands of similar stories. One particularly popular version is the concept of the "super co-op"—many small retailers within an industry band together to buy cooperatively. Their huge volume ensures them lower

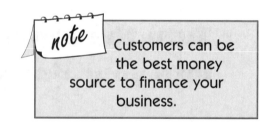

note
Customers can be the best money source to finance your business.

prices, better terms, and the profits needed to compete against national chains. The retailers contribute capital to join the co-op, which then purchases merchandise for its members.

The ABC's of inventory financing

Another way to finance your down payment is to look for excess inventory that can be quickly sold without hurting the business. Suggest that instead of your down payment, the seller sell the excess inventory and apply the proceeds to his down payment. A common variation is the "simultaneous sell-off" where a buyer in a similar business buys the excess inventory once you buy the business. Many businesses have more inventory than they need to maintain sales. Your down payment may be sitting on the shelf.

Financing from cash flow

One great way to raise your down payment is to squeeze the business' cash flow. The average business does enough business in two or three weeks to cover its down payment. Your strategy then is to have this cash flow finance the down payment after you buy the business.

First, calculate surplus cash flow by subtracting projected expenses from cash receipts over the first several weeks. This is cash available to pay to the seller for the down payment. Project conservatively. Underestimate, don't overestimate, the available money.

To maximize cash flow, defer every possible expense. Forecast how long you can delay suppliers. Return excess or unsalable merchandise to vendors for credit. Negotiate more lenient credit terms with suppliers. Every dollar in credit is a dollar you can offer the seller for the down payment.

Or convince the seller to withhold payments to his suppliers. The business' debts may rise, but the seller can take this cash for the down payment. You will assume and eventually pay these supplier debts but for now you have a business with no cash down.

Remember, while every seller wants an all-cash deal, sellers don't care where the money comes from. Borrow from a bank, relatives, creditors, or even the seller's own business. Just get him the cash.

To make the seller more comfortable with cash flow financing, hand him post-dated checks for the down payment. This gives the seller no more legal protection than a short-term promissory note, but a check is psychologically comforting. People are wary of promissory notes and will more likely respect your personal check as payment in hand.

The sale-leaseback strategy

Equipment and real estate also can generate your down payment via a sale-leaseback. Example: A small family owned pool-cleaning service sold for $100,000. Its assets included four trucks and equipment worth $50,000, and the good will from 100 accounts generating seasonal revenues of $150,000. The seller asked $100,000 for the business with $35,000 down. At the closing the buyer sold the trucks to investors for $35,000 who then leased the trucks to the buyer for $700 per month. The buyer had his $35,000 down payment from the seller's trucks.

The sale-leaseback works with any type equipment or even real estate, but computers, high technology items, material handling equipment, and motor vehicles are prime assets for a sale-leaseback.

Or why not time-share your business? Time-sharing under-used equipment is another way to a down payment. Suppose the business has a computer or printing press that is seldom used. Why not rent it to others when its not working for you? If your equipment can handle two or three times the work you demand from it, you may be able to collect substantial rents by leasing it to others. Time-sharing gets you your down payment if your time sharing customers will prepay their rental fee. Offer them a substantial prepayment discount. The customer saves money, and you have your down payment.

The business asset to target may be neither its inventory nor equipment, but its lease. The right location can turn any businesses into a money-machine for a down payment. How? Enter into an advance agreement to sublease part of your space, and collect advance rent (offer a discount if necessary). It has worked for countless entrepreneurs. Only your imagination limits the possibilities.

Idle space can produce big results. Do you have billboard space? Negotiate a lease with a major billboard company. They pay big advances. Do you have an idle parking lot? Turn it into immediate cash. For example, an evening restaurant might profitably lease the lot during the day.

Turn accounts receivable into fast cash

Accounts receivable is cash that flows into your business. Therefore, if your target business has $20,000 in receivables, and the seller wants $20,000 for a down payment you can see two immediate solutions: Give the seller the accounts receivable in place of the down payment (the receivables will generate cash for the seller in 30 to 60 days and you will not have to collect yourself) or "factor" the accounts receivable. A factor buys your receivables for about 90 percent of their face value. Turning this "immediate" cash over to the seller decreases the down payment you need.

Partners for profit

If you are an individual who wants to share responsibility and decisions—and can't raise money any other way—then consider a partner. But if you need only a partner's money, then move cautiously. Partnership money is mighty expensive money. Your partner's small investment may cost you many times that amount over the years. Beg or borrow money from wherever you can, but make a partner your last resort for raising capital.

> **HINT**
> Regardless of their number, or what they invest, all partners share one point: Once aboard, you work for them. You no longer work only for yourself.

If you do sincerely want a partner, then distinguish the good from the bad. Examine your potential partner's work history. Is it a solid work record? Is he a "doer" or a "drifter"? Does he have needed management skills? Does he command your confidence? Look for stability. And what about your future partner's personal history? Poor health can pose major problems, as can personal weaknesses, such as gambling or drinking.

Investigate all the skeletons in his closet. Has he been in other business deals? How did they work out? What do his prior partners say about him? And what about personal lifestyles? A clash of lifestyles can cause huge partnership problems. And evaluate your partner's spouse. Spouses influence their mates. A perfect partner may have an interfering spouse. That can destroy the partnership.

Can your partner match your financial resources? He may match your down payment but can he raise the money to help the business grow? Why mortgage your house because your partner has nothing to offer? Be as careful with a partner considerably wealthier than yourself. You may find yourself on the short end of a squeeze play. You may be the brains behind the business, but money always wins. Finally, are your ideas compatible concerning growth, responsibility, and finances?

Your partner may be a close college friend or business acquaintance. You may have answered a newspaper ad from someone with capital to invest. Or perhaps placed your own an ad for a partner. Whenever you approach someone for money, you must sell him on your business idea. Whether starting from scratch or buying an existing business, you need a business proposal that contains:

1) **Company background:** Its history, organization, current financial statements, and legal structure (sole proprietorship, corporation, etc.)

2) **Management:** Their backgrounds and accomplishments. Show that the company has effective management. For investors, good management is as important as a good business concept.

3) **Competitive advantages:** Outline why the company, product, or service is unique.

4) **Competition:** Analyze your competitors. How do their products compare with yours?

5) **Marketing:** Identify your market segment. Who are your customers? Describe advertising, promotion and sales costs. Detail how your product is distributed to your markets.

6) **Finances:** Project your financial statements over several years. Work with an accountant on this.

7) **Investment:** How will you use the money you seek? Will additional funds be needed and where will it come from? How will you raise money for expansion?

8) **The deal:** Sell the investment in terms of safety, return on investment, and growth potential.

Review your proposal. Can you back it up with hard facts? To discover how much you really know about your business, investors will try to pick your plan apart. They won't open their wallets unless you can convince them that you know your business.

Also create a formula to buy out your partner if you should disagree. Demand at least 51 percent ownership for voting control. If your partner insists on a 50-50 deal, try to obtain voting control by having your partner assign to you the right to vote some of his shares.

Join the franchise boom

Franchisers routinely finance 60-70 percent of the start-up cost. They may also guarantee your bank loan or make a direct loan. However, the better franchise systems demand excellent credit from their franchisees.

note | Financing is one big benefit of joining a franchise system.

Because a franchiser can easily reclaim a mismanaged franchised business, a franchiser can offer more generous finance terms. If the franchiser offers a $120,000 package with $20,000 down and financing for $100,000, you can be certain the franchiser can resell the business for $100,000 if you don't make the grade.

Real estate financing

Using real estate as collateral whether your own or someone else's is an excellent way to finance a business.

- Mortgage companies represent the largest pool of lenders. They will be able to match your commercial property with a lender specializing in that particular type of property.

- Life insurance companies and pension funds are active in the larger real estate markets, usually specializing in expensive properties.

- Finance companies may charge higher rates but do provide smaller loans on commercial property.

Be sure to shop around and interview as many different sources as is practical. They all have different policies and specialize in different areas of the marketplace.

Taxation

Taxation

10

After you have incorporated, there are several government programs involving source deductions and taxes in which you may have to participate. Depending on your particular business, you may not require registration in all programs.

If you sell items subject to Retail Sales Tax you must submit the RST that you collect to the government. If you sell items subject to the Goods and Services Tax, you may have to submit GST payments to the federal government. If your corporation has employees, you must remit Unemployment Insurance premiums, Canada Pension Plan deductions and Income Tax deductions to the federal government. You will also be required to submit Employee Health Tax premiums and Workers Compensation Board premiums to the government.

Corporate taxes

A lower small business tax rate applies to the first $200,000 of business income earned by Canadian corporations. Also, manufacturing and processing corporations qualify for a special tax rate on certain income. Different forms of income, such as interest, royalties, income from foreign

> *note* Corporate income tax rates vary depending on the type of business and its net income.

subsidiaries, capital gains and dividends, are treated differently, making corporate business taxes complicated and constantly changing. The following are a few tax tips to remember:

- Depending on when you start operations, your corporation may have a taxation year other than the calendar year.

- Corporate taxes must be paid by monthly installments, based on either a tax payable estimate for the year or the tax paid the previous year.

You should open a corporate tax installment account with Canada Customs and Revenue Agency as soon as your business operations begin.

- Corporate residents in specified provinces must submit income tax returns separately to the federal and provincial governments. Please check with your provincial office.

- Corporate assets such as buildings, vehicles and equipment are not deducted from income in the same way as other expenses.

- Profits and losses may be offset over a seven year period. Business losses may be carried back one year or carried forward five years when calculating taxable income.

GST/HST?

Goods and Services Tax is a 7% tax on the supply of most goods and services in Canada. Three participating provinces (Nova Scotia, New Brunswick, and Newfoundland) harmonized their provincial sales tax with GST to create the harmonized sales tax (HST). HST applies to the same base of goods and services as GST, but at the rate of 15%. Of this, 7% is the federal part and 8% is the provincial part.

GST/HST registrants who make taxable sales of goods and services (other than zero-rated sales) in the three participating provinces collect tax at the 15% HST rate. They collect tax at the 7% GST rate on taxable sales of goods and services they make in the rest of Canada (other than zero-rated sales).

Who pays GST/HST?

> note
>
> As a GST/HST registrant, you charge 7% GST or 15% HST on the taxable goods and services you provide (other than zero-rated).

Almost everyone has to pay GST at 7% or HST at 15% on taxable sales of goods and services (other than zero-rated sales). The only groups or organizations that do not always pay GST/HST on their purchases are provincial and territorial governments and Indians.

Taxable goods and services

Examples of goods and services taxable at 7% or 15% include:

- commercial real property and newly constructed residential real property

- rentals of commercial real property

- sales and leases of automobiles

- gasoline

- car repairs

- soft drinks, candies, and potato chips

- clothing and footwear

- advertising (unless provided to a non-resident of Canada who is not registered for GST/HST)

- taxi and limousine fares

- legal and accounting fees

- franchise fees

- hotel accommodation

- barber and hairstylist services

Examples of goods and services taxable at 0% (zero-rated) include:

- basic groceries such as milk, bread, and vegetables

- agricultural products such as grain, raw wool, and dried tobacco leaves

- most farm livestock

- most fishery products such as fish for human consumption

- prescription drugs and drug dispensing fees, medical devices such as hearing aids and artificial teeth

- exports (most goods and services taxable at 7% or 15% in Canada are zero-rated when exported)

Exempt goods and services. A small number of goods and services are exempt from GST/HST—that is, no GST/HST applies to them. Examples include:

- used residential housing

- long-term residential accommodation (of one month or more), and residential condominium fees

- most health, medical, and dental services performed by licensed physicians or dentists for medical reasons

- child-care services (day-care services provided usually for less than 24 hours a day) provided primarily to children 14 years old and younger

- bridge, road, and ferry tolls (ferry tolls are zero-rated if the ferry service is to or from a place outside Canada)

- legal aid services

- many educational services such as courses supplied by a vocational school leading to a certificate or a diploma which allow the practice of a trade or a vocation, or tutoring services made to an individual in a course that follows a curriculum designated by a school authority, music lessons

- most services provided by financial institutions such as arrangements for a loan or mortgage

> **HOT spot** Generally, if you provide only exempt goods and services, you cannot register for GST/HST or charge tax on your sales and services.

- arranging for and issuing insurance policies by insurance companies, agents, and brokers

- most goods and services provided by charities

- certain goods and services provided by non-profit organizations, governments, and other public service bodies, such as municipal transit services and standard residential services such as water distribution.

Should you register?

You have to register for GST/HST if:

- You provide taxable goods and services in Canada.

- You are not a small supplier.

- If you are a partnership or a corporation, the total taxable revenues of the partnership or corporation are $30,000 or less in the last four consecutive calendar quarters or in a single calendar quarter.

Excise tax

You must be licensed for Excise Tax if you are manufacturing goods subject to Excise Tax and your sales exceed $50,000.00 in a calendar year. Some examples of goods subject to Excise Tax are:

- clocks, watches

- jewellery

- gasoline

- tobacco

Payroll deductions

You are generally considered to be an employer if:

- you pay a salary, wages (including advances) bonuses, vacation pay, or tips to your employees

- you provide certain benefits, such as board and lodging to your employees.

An employer-employee relationship exists if you are in a position to control and direct the person or people who perform services. Although a written contract might expressly indicate that an individual is self-employed, Canada Customs and Revenue Agency might not necessarily consider the individual as such.

You must examine the written contract and the working conditions to determine if the individual is self-employed. If you cannot determine whether a person is an employee, you can obtain a ruling from the Trust Accounts Division of Canada Customs and Revenue Agency.

Employer responsibility

As an employer, you have to :

- ensure that you have a Business Number which identifies the four major Canada Customs and Revenue Agency business accounts:

    1) corporate income tax

    2) import/export

    3) payroll deductions

    4) goods and services tax (GST)

- deduct income tax, Canada Pension Plan (CPP) contributions, and Employment Insurance (EI) premiums from amounts you pay to your employees

- send in these amounts along with your share of CPP contributions and EI premiums that you have to pay throughout the year on your employees' behalf

- get a social insurance number from each employee and report all these amounts on an information return by the end of February of the following calendar year.

As an employer, you hold payroll deductions in trust for the Receiver General. Therefore, you have to keep these amounts separate from the operating funds of your business.

Eligibility criteria

Payers or workers want to know the nature of their business relationship. A payer's or a worker's responsibilities are different according to the type of employment relationship that exists. If the type of employment relationship is not correctly established from the beginning, there could be consequences for the payer and the worker.

To determine if a worker is an employee or a self-employed individual, and thus if there is an employer-employee relationship, or a business relationship, you have to examine and analyze the terms and conditions of the worker's employment as they relate to the following four factors:

- **Control.** Control is the most important factor. Generally, in an employer-employee relationship, the employer controls, directly or not, the way the work is done and the work methods used. The employer assigns specific tasks that define the real framework within which the work is to be done. If the employer does not directly control the worker's activities, but has the right to do so, the notion of control still exists.

Generally, the payer exercises control if he has the right to hire or fire, determines the wage or salary to be paid, and decides on the time, place, and manner in which the work is to be done. In a business relationship, conversely, the payer does not exercise control over the worker's activities. The worker can decide how the work will be performed.

- **Ownership of tools.** The main points to consider are:

    ° the amount invested

    ° the value of equipment and tools

    ° the rental and maintenance of equipment and tools

In an employer-employee relationship, the employer generally supplies the equipment and tools required by the employee. In addition, the employer covers the following costs related to their use:

° repairs

° insurance

° transport

° rental

° operation (e.g., fuel)

In some trades, however, it is customary for employees to supply their own tools. This is generally the case for garage mechanics, painters, and carpenters. Similarly, employed computer scientists, architects and surveyors sometimes supply their own software and instruments.

In a business relationship, workers generally supply their own equipment and tools and cover costs related to their use. When workers purchase or rent equipment or large tools that require a major investment and costly maintenance, it usually indicates that they are self-employed individuals, because they may incur losses when replacing or repairing their equipment.

- **Chance of Profit/Risk of Loss.** You must examine the worker's financial involvement. Determine if the worker:

  ° has the chance of making a profit

  ° risks losses due to bad debts, damage to equipment or materials, or unforeseen delivery delays

  ° covers operating costs

The employer generally covers operating costs, which may include office expenses, employee wages and benefits, insurance premiums, and delivery and shipping costs. The employee does not assume any financial risk and is entitled to his full salary or wages regardless of the financial health of the business.

In a business relationship, the self-employed individual may make a profit or incur a loss. He also covers operating costs. There is no guarantee of a steady income because the self-employed individual's income depends on the results achieved by the end of the contract.

> *note* Generally, in an employer-employee relationship, the employer alone assumes the risk of loss.

- **Integration.** Integration must be considered from the point of view of the worker, not the payer.

  ° Where the worker integrates the payer's activities to his own commercial activities, a business relationship probably exists. The worker is acting on his own behalf, he is not dependent on the payer's business and he is in business for himself.

  ° Where the worker integrates his activities to the commercial activities of the payer, an employer-employee relationship probably exists. The worker is acting on behalf of the employer, he is connected with the employer's business and is dependent on it.

Where an employer-employee relationship exists, the employer must:

- register for CCRA's Business Number (BN)

- withhold income tax, Canada Pension Plan (CPP) contributions, and Employment Insurance (EI) premiums on amounts paid to employees

- remit the amounts withheld as well as the required employer's share of CPP/QPP contributions and EI premiums to CCRA

- report the employees' income and deductions on the appropriate information return, and give the employees copies of their T4 slips by the end of February of the following calendar year.

The employer is also responsible for registering with the relevant provincial organizations if applicable (Workplace Safety and Insurance Board, WSIB, for example).

Where a business relationship exists, and where the self-employed individuals' income exceeds $500 or income tax has been deducted, the payer must:

- report the self-employed individuals' income and tax deductions, if any, on he appropriate information return

- give the self-employed individuals copies of their T4A slips by the end of February of the following calendar year, if applicable

Self-employed individuals must pay both shares of CPP/QPP contributions. They may also have to pay their income tax and CPP/QPP contributions in installments.

Special Situations

Special rules concerning EI, CPP/QPP and income tax may apply for certain categories of self-employed individuals, including:

- barbers and hairdressers

- drivers of taxis and other passenger-carrying vehicles

- fishermen

- placement and employment agency workers

Dissolving your corporation

Dissolving your corporation

There are many ways to dissolve a corporation, depending upon provincial law. A corporation may be dissolved by:

1) Expiration of the period specified in the corporate charter (Certificate of Incorporation), if any expiration date is stated.

2) A surrender of the charter. When the shareholders of a corporation, by majority vote, surrender the corporate charter to the province and it is formally accepted, the corporation is dissolved.

3) Filing the Articles of Dissolution with the Director, Canada Business Corporations Act, in the province of incorporation.

4) Consolidation. When Corporation A unites with Corporation B to form a third but entirely separate Corporation C, corporations A and B cease to exist and are said to have been dissolved "by consolidation." Corporation C assumes all the assets, property rights, privileges and liabilities of former corporations A and B.

5) Merger. When Corporation A merges into Corporation B, Corporation A is dissolved "by merger." Corporation B survives. The surviving corporation absorbs all the assets, property rights, privileges, and often the liabilities of the absorbed corporation, but continues its own separate corporate existence thereafter.

6) The occurrence of a condition. A corporation may be dissolved when a condition clearly specified in the corporate charter, such as the death of a principal, occurs. This provision is rare, however, as corporations have a perpetual life independent of their principals.

7) Legislative repeal. Under the inherent rights reserved by most provinces to "alter, amend, or repeal" the charter granted to a corporation, a legislature may, for some reason, find it necessary to revoke a corporate charter, thereby terminating the corporate existence. This is more commonly exercised with non-profit corporations.

8) Lawsuit. The province (and only the province) can sue to terminate the existence of a corporation. If satisfied that the province has proven its case (e.g., when the court finds that a corporation has not filed required taxes or documents or that it has abused or neglected to use its powers), the court may revoke the corporate charter.

9) Directors' or shareholders' petition. The board of directors (or a majority thereof) may be empowered by statute to petition for the dissolution of a corporation upon the occurrence of certain events, e.g., when the assets of the corporation are not sufficient to discharge its liabilities. The stockholders of a majority of all outstanding shares entitled to vote on the issue may also be empowered by statute to make such petition to the court on similar grounds.

10) Shareholders' petition under deadlock statutes. A "deadlock statute" commonly provides:

"Unless otherwise provided in the Articles of Incorporation, the holders of one-half of all outstanding shares of a corporation entitled to vote in an election of directors may present a petition for dissolution on one or more of the following grounds:

- The directors are so divided respecting the management of the corporation's affairs that the votes required for action by the board cannot be obtained.

- The shareholders are so divided that the votes required for the election of directors cannot be obtained.

- There is internal dissension and two or more factions of shareholders are so divided that dissolution would be beneficial to the shareholders."

The dissolution of a corporation carries with it important tax and liability questions, and therefore should be undertaken only after consulting with a lawyer and accountant.

The Forms In This Guide

MINUTE BOOK

_____

Insert Here

a copy of your filed

Articles/Certificate of Incorporation

Bylaws

of

_____

adopted_____

BYLAWS
OF

_____

ARTICLE I
OFFICES

The principal office of the Corporation in the Province of   shall be located in   , County of   . The Corporation may have such other offices, either within or without the Province of   , as the Board of Directors may designate or as the business of the Corporation may require from time to time.

ARTICLE II
SHAREHOLDERS

SECTION 1. Annual Meeting. The annual meeting of the shareholders shall be held on the   day in the month of   in each year, beginning with the year   , at the hour of   o'clock   .m., for the purpose of electing Directors and for the transaction of such other business as may come before the meeting. If the day fixed for the annual meeting shall be a legal holiday in the Province of   , such meeting shall be held on the next succeeding business day. If the election of Directors shall not be held on the day designated herein for any annual meeting of the shareholders, or at any adjournment thereof, the Board of Directors shall cause the election to be held at a special meeting of the shareholders as soon thereafter as conveniently may be.

SECTION 2. Special Meetings. Special meetings of the shareholders, for any purpose or purposes, unless otherwise prescribed by statute, may be called by the President or by the Board of Directors, and shall be called by the President at the request of the holders of not less than   percent (%) of all the outstanding shares of the Corporation entitled to vote at the meeting.

SECTION 3. Place of Meeting. The Board of Directors may designate any place, either within or without the Province of   , unless otherwise prescribed by statute, as the place of meeting for any annual meeting or for any special meeting. A waiver of notice signed by all shareholders entitled to vote at a meeting may designate any place, either within or without the Province of   , unless otherwise prescribed by statute, as the place for the holding of such meeting. If no designation is made, the place of meeting shall be the principal office of the Corporation.

SECTION 4. Notice of Meeting. Written notice stating the place, day and hour of the meeting and, in case of a special meeting, the purpose or purposes for which the meeting is called, shall unless otherwise prescribed by statute, be delivered not less than   (   ) nor more than   (   ) days before the date of the meeting, to each shareholder of record entitled to vote at such meeting. If mailed, such notice shall be deemed to be delivered when deposited in the mail, addressed to the shareholder at his/her address as it appears on the stock transfer books of the Corporation, with postage thereon prepaid.

SECTION 5. <u>Closing of Transfer Books or Fixing of Record</u>. For the purpose of determining shareholders entitled to notice of or to vote at any meeting of shareholders or any adjournment thereof, or shareholders entitled to receive payment of any dividend, or in order to make a determination of shareholders for any other proper purpose, the Board of Directors of the Corporation may provide that the stock transfer books shall be closed for a stated period, but not to exceed in any case fifty (50) days. If the stock transfer books shall be closed for the purpose of determining shareholders entitled to notice of or to vote at a meeting of shareholders, such books shall be closed for at least   (   ) days immediately preceding such meeting. In lieu of closing the stock transfer books, the Board of Directors may fix in advance a date as the record date for any such determination of shareholders, such date in any case to be not more than   (   ) days and, in case of a meeting of shareholders, not less than   (   ) days, prior to the date on which the particular action requiring such determination of shareholders is to be taken. If the stock transfer books are not closed and no record date is fixed for the determination of shareholders entitled to notice of or to vote at a meeting of shareholders, or shareholders entitled to receive payment of a dividend, the date on which notice of the meeting is mailed or the date on which the resolution of the Board of Directors declaring such dividend is adopted, as the case may be, shall be the record date for such determination of shareholders. When a determination of shareholders entitled to vote at any meeting of shareholders has been made as provided in this section, such determination shall apply to any adjournment thereof.

SECTION 6. <u>Voting Lists</u>. The officer or agent having charge of the stock transfer books for shares of the corporation shall make a complete list of the shareholders entitled to vote at each meeting of shareholders or any adjournment thereof, arranged in alphabetical order, with the address of and the number of shares held by each. Such list shall be produced and kept open at the time and place of the meeting and shall be subject to the inspection of any shareholder during the whole time of the meeting for the purposes thereof.

SECTION 7. <u>Quorum</u>. A majority of the outstanding shares of the Corporation entitled to vote, represented in person or by proxy, shall constitute a quorum at a meeting of shareholders. If less than a majority of the outstanding shares are represented at a meeting, a majority of the shares so represented may adjourn the meeting from time to time without further notice. At such adjourned meeting at which a quorum shall be present or represented, any business may be transacted which might have been transacted at the meeting as originally noticed. The shareholders present at a duly organized meeting may continue to transact business until adjournment, notwithstanding the withdrawal of enough shareholders to leave less than a quorum.

SECTION 8. <u>Proxies</u>. At all meetings of shareholders, a shareholder may vote in person or by proxy executed in writing by the shareholder or by his/her duly authorized attorney-in-fact. Such proxy shall be filed with the secretary of the Corporation before or at the time of the meeting. A meeting of the Board of Directors may be had by means of a telephone conference or similar communications equipment by which all persons participating in the meeting can hear each other, and participation in a meeting under such circumstances shall constitute presence at the meeting.

SECTION 9. <u>Voting of Shares</u>. Each outstanding share entitled to vote shall be entitled to one vote upon each matter submitted to a vote at a meeting of shareholders.

SECTION 10. <u>Voting of Shares by Certain Holders</u>. Shares standing in the name of another corporation may be voted by such officer, agent or proxy as the Bylaws of such corporation may prescribe or, in the absence of such provision, as the Board of Directors of such corporation may determine. Shares held by an administrator, executor, guardian or conservator may be voted by him, either in person or by proxy, without a transfer of such shares into his name. Shares standing in the name of a trustee may be voted by him, either in person or by proxy, but no trustee shall be entitled to vote shares held by him without a transfer of such shares into his name.

Shares standing in the name of a receiver may be voted by such receiver, and shares held by or under the control of a receiver may be voted by such receiver without the transfer thereof into his name, if authority so to do be contained in an appropriate order of the court by which such receiver was appointed.

A shareholder whose shares are pledged shall be entitled to vote such shares until the shares have been transferred into the name of the pledgee, and thereafter the pledgee shall be entitled to vote the shares so transferred.

Shares of its own stock belonging to the Corporation shall not be voted, directly or indirectly, at any meeting, and shall not be counted in determining the total number of outstanding shares at any given time.

SECTION 11. Informal Action by Shareholders. Unless otherwise provided by law, any action required to be taken at a meeting of the shareholders, or any other action which may be taken at a meeting of the shareholders, may be taken without a meeting if a consent in writing, setting forth the action so taken, shall be signed by all of the shareholders entitled to vote with respect to the subject matter thereof.

ARTICLE III
BOARD OF DIRECTORS

SECTION 1. General Powers. The business and affairs of the Corporation shall be managed by its Board of Directors.

SECTION 2. Number, Tenure and Qualifications. The number of directors of the Corporation shall be fixed by the Board of Directors, but in no event shall be less than   ( ). Each director shall hold office until the next annual meeting of shareholders and until his/her successor shall have been elected and qualified.

SECTION 3. Regular Meetings. A regular meeting of the Board of Directors shall be held without other notice than this Bylaw immediately after, and at the same place as, the annual meeting of shareholders. The Board of Directors may provide, by resolution, the time and place for the holding of additional regular meetings without notice other than such resolution.

SECTION 4. Special Meetings. Special meetings of the Board of Directors may be called by or at the request of the President or any two directors. The person or persons authorized to call special meetings of the Board of Directors may fix the place for holding any special meeting of the Board of Directors called by them.

SECTION 5. Notice. Notice of any special meeting shall be given at least one (1) day previous thereto by written notice delivered personally or mailed to each director at his business address, or by telegram. If mailed, such notice shall be deemed to be delivered when deposited in the mail so addressed, with postage thereon prepaid. If notice be given by telegram, such notice shall be deemed to be delivered when the telegram is delivered to the telegraph company. Any directors may waive notice of any meeting. The attendance of a director at a meeting shall constitute a waiver of notice of such meeting, except where a director attends a meeting for the express purpose of objecting to the transaction of any business because the meeting is not lawfully called or convened.

SECTION 6. Quorum. A majority of the number of directors fixed by Section 2 of this Article III shall constitute a quorum for the transaction of business at any meeting of the Board of Directors, but if less than such majority is present at a meeting, a majority of the directors present may adjourn the meeting from time to time without further notice.

SECTION 7. Manner of Acting. The act of the majority of the directors present at a meeting at which a quorum is present shall be the act of the Board of Directors.

SECTION 8. Action Without a Meeting. Any action that may be taken by the Board of Directors at a meeting may be taken without a meeting if a consent in writing, setting forth the action so to be taken, shall be signed before such action by all of the directors.

SECTION 9. Vacancies. Any vacancy occurring in the Board of Directors may be filled by the affirmative vote of a majority of the remaining directors though less than a quorum of the Board of Directors, unless otherwise provided by law. A director elected to fill a vacancy shall be elected for the unexpired term of his/her predecessor in office. Any directorship to be filled by reason of an increase in the number of directors may be filled by election by the Board of Directors for a term of office continuing only until the next election of directors by the shareholders.

SECTION 10. Compensation. By resolution of the Board of Directors, each director may be paid his/her expenses, if any, of attendance at each meeting of the Board of Directors, and may be paid a stated salary as director or a fixed sum for attendance at each meeting of the Board of Directors or both. No such payment shall preclude any director from serving the Corporation in any other capacity and receiving compensation therefor.

SECTION 11. Presumption of Assent. A director of the Corporation who is present at a meeting of the Board of Directors at which action on any corporate matter is taken shall be presumed to have assented to the action taken unless his/her dissent shall be entered in the minutes of the meeting or unless he/she shall file written dissent to such action with the person acting as the Secretary of the meeting before the adjournment thereof, or shall forward such dissent by registered mail to the Secretary of the Corporation immediately after the adjournment of the meeting. Such right to dissent shall not apply to a director who voted in favor of such action.

ARTICLE IV
OFFICERS

SECTION 1. Number. The officers of the Corporation shall be a President, one or more Vice Presidents, a Secretary, and a Treasurer, each of whom shall be elected by the Board of Directors. Such other officers and assistant officers as may be deemed necessary may be elected or appointed by the Board of Directors, including a Chairman of the Board. In its discretion, the Board of Directors may leave unfilled for any such period as it may determine any office except those of President and Secretary. Any two or more offices may be held by the same person, except for the offices of President and Secretary which may not be held by the same person. Officers may be directors or shareholders of the Corporation.

SECTION 2. Election and Term of Office. The officers of the Corporation to be elected by the Board of Directors shall be elected annually by the Board of Directors at the first meeting of the Board of Directors held after each annual meeting of the shareholders. If the election of officers shall not be held at such meeting, such election shall be held as soon thereafter as conveniently may be. Each officer shall hold office until his/her successor shall have been duly elected and shall have qualified, or until his/her death, or until he/she shall resign or shall have been removed in the manner hereinafter provided.

SECTION 3. Removal. Any officer or agent may be removed by the Board of Directors whenever, in its judgement, the best interests of the Corporation will be served thereby, but such removal shall be without prejudice to the contract rights, if any, of the person so removed. Election or appointment of an officer or agent shall not of itself create contract rights, and such appointment shall be terminable at will.

SECTION 4. Vacancies. A vacancy in any office because of death, resignation, removal, disqualification or otherwise, may be filled by the Board of Directors for the unexpired portion of the term.

SECTION 5. President. The President shall be the principal executive officer of the Corporation and, subject to the control of the Board of Directors, shall in general supervise and control all of the business and affairs of the Corporation. He/she shall, when present, preside at all meetings of the shareholders and of the Board of Directors, unless there is a Chairman of the Board, in which case the Chairman shall preside. The President may sign, with the Secretary or any other proper officer of the Corporation thereunto authorized by the Board of Directors, certificates for shares of the Corporation, any deeds, mortgages, bonds, contracts, or other instruments which the Board of Directors has authorized to be executed, except in cases where the signing and execution thereof   shall   be expressly delegated by the Board of Directors or by these Bylaws to some other officer or agent of the Corporation, or shall be required by law to be otherwise signed or executed; and in general shall perform all duties incident to the office of President and such other duties as may be prescribed by the Board of Directors from time to time.

SECTION 6. Vice President. In the absence of the President or in event of his/her death, inability or refusal to act, the Vice President shall perform the duties of the President, and when so acting, shall have all the powers of and be subject to all the restrictions upon the President. The Vice President shall perform such other duties as from time to time may be assigned by the President or by the Board of Directors. If there is more than one Vice President, each Vice President shall succeed to the duties of the President in order of rank as determined by the Board of Directors. If no such rank has been determined, then each Vice President shall succeed to the duties of the President in order of date of election, the earliest date having the first rank.

SECTION 7. Secretary. The Secretary shall: (a) keep the minutes of the proceedings of the shareholders and of the Board of Directors in one or more minute books provided for that purpose; (b) see that all notices are duly given in accordance with the provisions of these Bylaws or as required by law; (c) be custodian of the corporate records and of the seal of the Corporation and see that the seal of the Corporation is affixed to all documents, the execution of which on behalf of the

Corporation under its seal is duly authorized; (d) keep a register of the post office address of each shareholder which shall be furnished to the Secretary by such shareholder; (e) sign with the President certificates for shares of the Corporation, the issuance of which shall have been authorized by resolution of the Board of Directors; (f) have general charge of the stock transfer books of the Corporation; and (g) in general perform all duties incident to the office of the Secretary and such other duties as from time to time may be assigned by the President or by the Board of Directors.

SECTION 8. <u>Treasurer</u>. The Treasurer shall: (a) have charge and custody of and be responsible for all funds and securities of the Corporation; (b) receive and give receipts for moneys due and payable to the Corporation from any source whatsoever, and deposit all such moneys in the name of the Corporation in such banks, trust companies or other depositories as shall be selected in accordance with the provisions of Article VI of these Bylaws; and (c) in general perform all of the duties incident to the office of Treasurer and such other duties as from time to time may be assigned to him by the President or by the Board of Directors. If required by the Board of Directors, the Treasurer shall give a bond for the faithful discharge of his/her duties in such sum and with such sureties as the Board of Directors shall determine.

SECTION 9. <u>Salaries</u>. The salaries of the officers shall be fixed from time to time by the Board of Directors, and no officer shall be prevented from receiving such salary by reason of the fact that he/she is also a director of the Corporation.

ARTICLE V
INDEMNITY

The Corporation shall indemnify its directors, officers and employees as follows:

(a) Every director, officer, or employee of the Corporation shall be indemnified by the Corporation against all expenses and liabilities, including counsel fees, reasonably incurred by or imposed upon him/her in connection with any proceeding to which he/she may be made a party, or in which he/she may become involved, by reason of being or having been a director, officer, employee or agent of the Corporation or is or was serving at the request of the Corporation as a director, officer, employee or agent of the corporation, partnership, joint venture, trust or enterprise, or any settlement thereof, whether or not he/she is a director, officer, employee or agent at the time such expenses are incurred, except in such cases wherein the director, officer, or employee is adjudged guilty of willful misfeasance or malfeasance in the performance of his/her duties; provided that in the event of a settlement the indemnification herein shall apply only when the Board of Directors approves such settlement and reimbursement as being for the best interests of the Corporation.

(b) The Corporation shall provide to any person who is or was a director, officer, employee, or agent of the Corporation or is or was serving at the request of the Corporation as a director, officer, employee or agent of the corporation, partnership, joint venture, trust or enterprise, the indemnity against expenses of suit, litigation or other proceedings which is specifically permissible under applicable law.

(c) The Board of Directors may, in its discretion, direct the purchase of liability insurance by way of implementing the provisions of this Article V.

ARTICLE VI
CONTRACTS, LOANS, CHEQUES, AND DEPOSITS

SECTION 1. Contracts. The Board of Directors may authorize any officer or officers, agent or agents, to enter into any contract or execute and deliver any instrument in the name of and on behalf of the Corporation, and such authority may be general or confined to specific instances.

SECTION 2. Loans. No loans shall be contracted on behalf of the Corporation and no evidences of indebtedness shall be issued in its name unless authorized by a resolution of the Board of Directors. Such authority may be general or confined to specific instances.

SECTION 3. Cheques, Drafts, etc. All cheques, drafts or other orders for the payment of money, notes or other evidences of indebtedness issued in the name of the Corporation, shall be signed by such officer or officers, agent or agents of the Corporation and in such manner as shall from time to time be determined by resolution of the Board of Directors.

SECTION 4. Deposits. All funds of the Corporation not otherwise employed shall be deposited from time to time to the credit of the Corporation in such banks, trust companies or other depositories as the Board of Directors may select.

ARTICLE VII
CERTIFICATES FOR SHARES AND THEIR TRANSFER

SECTION 1. Certificates for Shares. Certificates representing shares of the Corporation shall be in such form as shall be determined by the Board of Directors. Such certificates shall be signed by the President and by the Secretary or by such other officers authorized by law and by the Board of Directors so to do, and sealed with the corporate seal. All certificates for shares shall be consecutively numbered or otherwise identified. The name and address of the person to whom the shares represented thereby are issued, with the number of shares and date of issue, shall be entered on the stock transfer books of the Corporation. All certificates surrendered to the Corporation for transfer shall be cancelled and no new certificate shall be issued until the former certificate for a like number of shares shall have been surrendered and cancelled, except that in case of a lost, destroyed or mutilated certificate, a new one may be issued therefor upon such terms and indemnity to the Corporation as the Board of Directors may prescribe.

SECTION 2. Transfer of Shares. Transfer of shares of the Corporation shall be made only on the stock transfer books of the Corporation by the holder of record thereof or by his/her legal representative, who shall furnish proper evidence of authority to transfer, or by his/her attorney thereunto authorized by power of attorney duly executed and filed with the Secretary of the Corporation, and on surrender for cancellation of the certificate for such shares. The person in whose name shares stand on the books of the Corporation shall be deemed by the Corporation to be the owner thereof for all purposes.

ARTICLE VIII
FISCAL YEAR

The fiscal year of the Corporation shall begin on the   day of   and end on the   day of   of each year.

ARTICLE IX
DIVIDENDS

The Board of Directors may from time to time declare, and the Corporation may pay, dividends on its outstanding shares in the manner and upon the terms and conditions provided by law and its Articles of Incorporation.

ARTICLE X
CORPORATE SEAL

The Board of Directors shall provide a corporate seal which shall be circular in form and shall have inscribed thereon the name of the Corporation and the province of incorporation and the words, "Corporate Seal."

ARTICLE XI
WAIVER OF NOTICE

Unless otherwise provided by law, whenever any notice is required to be given to any shareholder or director of the Corporation under the provisions of these Bylaws or under the provisions of the Articles of Incorporation or under the provisions of the applicable Business Corporation Act, a waiver thereof in writing, signed by the person or persons entitled to such notice, whether before or after the time stated therein, shall be deemed equivalent to the giving of such notice.

ARTICLE XII
AMENDMENTS

These Bylaws may be altered, amended or repealed and new Bylaws may be adopted by the Board of Directors at any regular or special meeting of the Board of Directors.

The above Bylaws are certified to have been adopted by the Board of Directors of the Corporation on the   day of   , 20   .

_____
Secretary

WAIVER OF NOTICE OF MEETING
OF INCORPORATORS AND DIRECTORS OF

_____

      We the undersigned do hereby constitute all the incorporators and directors of the above-named corporation and do hereby waive notice as to time and place of the first meeting of incorporators and directors of the aforesaid corporation.

      Furthermore, we hereby consent and agree that said meeting shall be held at
o'clock   .m. on   , 20   at the following place:

_____

      We do hereby affix our names to show our waiver of notice of said meeting.

_____   _____

_____   _____

_____   _____

_____   _____

Dated:

NOTICE OF ORGANIZATION MEETING
OF INCORPORATORS AND DIRECTORS

TO: _____

_____

_____

PLEASE BE ADVISED THAT:

We, the undersigned, do hereby constitute a majority of the directors named in the Articles of Incorporation of _____, a corporation;

Pursuant to provincial law, we are hereby calling an organization meeting of the Board of Directors and incorporators named in the Articles of Incorporation of the above named corporation for the purpose of adopting bylaws, electing officers, and transacting such other business as may come before the meeting; and

Said organization meeting shall be held at_____

_____

on _____, 20 ___, at _____ o'clock ___.m.

_____   _____

_____   _____

_____   _____

RECEIPT OF NOTICE

_____   _____
Addressee-Director   Date Received

153

MINUTES OF ORGANIZATION MEETING
OF BOARD OF DIRECTORS OF

_____

The organizational meeting of the Board of Directors of
was held at
on   , 20   , at   :   .m. Present were:

_____   _____

_____   _____

_____   _____

being persons designated as the Directors in the Articles of Incorporation.

Absent from the meeting were:

_____   _____

_____   _____

_____   _____

                                                                acted as temporary Chairman of the meeting
and
                                                                acted as temporary Secretary.

The Chairman announced that the meeting had been duly called by the Incorporators of the Corporation.

The Chairman reported that the Articles of Incorporation of the Corporation had been duly filed with the Province of   on   , 20   . The Certificate of Incorporation and a copy of said Articles of Incorporation were ordered to be inserted in the Minutes as a part of the records of the meeting.

A proposed form of Bylaws for the regulation and the management of the affairs of the Corporation was then presented at the meeting. The Bylaws were read and considered and, upon motion duly made and seconded, it was:

RESOLVED, that the form of Bylaws of the Corporation, as presented to this meeting, a copy of which is directed to be inserted in the Minute Book of the Corporation be, and the same are hereby approved and adopted as, the Bylaws of the Corporation.

The following persons were nominated officers of the Corporation to serve until their respective successors are chosen and qualify:

PRESIDENT:
VICE PRESIDENT:
SECRETARY:
TREASURER:

The Chairman announced that the aforenamed persons had been elected to the office set opposite their respective names.

The President thereupon took the chair and the Secretary immediately assumed the discharge of the duties of that office.

The President then stated that there were a number of organizational matters to be considered at the meeting and a number of resolutions to be adopted by the Board of Directors.

The form of stock certificates was then exhibited at the meeting. Thereupon, a motion duly made and seconded, it was:

RESOLVED, that the form of stock certificates presented at this meeting be, and the same is hereby adopted and approved as, the stock certificate of the Corporation, a specimen copy of the stock certificate to be inserted with these Minutes.

FURTHER RESOLVED, that the officers are hereby authorized to pay or reimburse the payment of all fees and expenses incident to and necessary for the organization of this Corporation.

The Board of Directors then considered the opening of a corporate bank account to serve as a depository for the funds of the Corporation. Following discussion, on motion duly made and seconded, it was:

RESOLVED, that the Treasurer be authorized, empowered and directed to open an account with and to deposit all funds of the Corporation, all drafts, cheques and notes of the Corporation, payable on said account to be made in the corporate name signed by

.

FURTHER RESOLVED, that officers are hereby authorized to execute such resolutions (including formal Bank Resolutions), documents and other instruments as may be necessary or advisable in opening or continuing said bank account. A copy of the applicable printed form of Bank Resolution hereby adopted to supplement these Minutes is ordered appended to the Minutes of this meeting.

It is announced that the following persons have offered to transfer the property listed below in exchange for the following shares of the stock of the Corporation:

Name	Payment Consideration, or Property	Number of Shares

Upon motion duly made and seconded, it was:

RESOLVED, that acceptance of the offer of the above-named stock subscribers is in the best interest of the Corporation and necessary for carrying out the corporate business, and in the judgment of the Board of Directors, the assets proposed to be transferred to the Corporation are reasonably worth the amount of consideration deemed therefor, and the same hereby is accepted, and that upon receipt of the consideration indicated above, the President and the Secretary are authorized to issue certificates of fully-paid, non-assessable capital stock of this Corporation in the amounts indicated to the above-named persons.

In order to provide for the payment of expenses of incorporation and organization of the Corporation, on motion duly made, seconded and unanimously carried, the following resolution was adopted:

RESOLVED, that the President and the Secretary and/or Treasurer of this Corporation be and they are hereby authorized and directed to pay the expenses of this Corporation, including lawyer's fees for incorporation, and to reimburse the persons who have made disbursements thereof.

After consideration of the pertinent issues with regard to the tax year and accounting basis, on motion duly made, and seconded and unanimously carried, the following resolution was adopted:

RESOLVED, that the first fiscal year of the Corporation shall commence on
            ,   and end on   ,   .

FURTHER RESOLVED, that the President be and is hereby authorized and directed to enter into employment contracts with certain employees, such contract shall be for the term and the rate stated in the attached Employment Agreements.

FURTHER RESOLVED, that it shall be the policy of the Corporation to reimburse each employee or to pay directly on his behalf all expenses incidental to his attendance at conventions and seminars as may be approved by the President. Reimbursement shall include full reimbursement for commercial and private transportation expenses, plus other necessary and ordinary out-of-pocket expenses incidental to the said travel, including meals and lodging.

A general discussion was then held concerning the immediate commencement of business operations as a Corporation and it was determined that business operations of the Corporation would commence as of   ,   . It was agreed that no fixed date would be set for holding meetings of the Board of Directors except the regular meetings to be held immediately after the annual meetings of shareholders as provided in the Bylaws of the Corporation, but that meetings of the Directors would be periodically called by the President and Secretary or others as provided by the Bylaws. Upon motion duly made, seconded and unanimously carried, it was:

RESOLVED, that the officers of the Corporation are hereby authorized to do any and all things necessary to conduct the business of the Corporation as set forth in the Articles of

Incorporation and Bylaws of the Corporation.

Upon motion duly made, seconded, and unanimously carried the following resolution was adopted:

RESOLVED, that, if required,
be, and hereby is, appointed Resident Agent in the Province of
.

The office of the Resident Agent will be located at

.

After a discussion, the following preamble was stated and the following resolution was unanimously:

RESOLVED, THAT:

(a) The plan as hereafter set forth shall, upon its adoption by the Board of Directors of the Corporation, immediately become effective.

(b) No more than   shares of common stock are authorized to be issued under this plan, such stock to have a par value of $ per share.

(c) Stock authorized under this plan shall be issued only in exchange for money, or property susceptible to monetary valuation other than capital stock, securities or services rendered or to be rendered. The aggregate dollar amount to be received for such stock shall not exceed $1,000,000, and the sum of each aggregate dollar amount and the equity capital of the Corporation (determined on the date of adoption of the plan) shall not exceed $1,000,000.

(d) Any stock options granted during the life of this plan which apply to the stock issuable hereunder shall apply solely to such stock and to no other and must be exercised within the period in which the plan is effective.

NOW, THEREFORE, the foregoing plan to issue Stock is adopted by the Corporation and the appropriate officers of the Corporation are authorized and directed to take all actions deemed by them necessary to carry out the intent and purpose of the recited plan.

There being no further business requiring Board action or consideration, on motion duly made, seconded and carried, the meeting was adjourned.

Dated:

_____
Secretary of the Meeting

WAIVER OF NOTICE,
FIRST MEETING OF SHAREHOLDERS

We the undersigned, being the shareholders of the
_____, agree that the first meeting of shareholders be on the date and at the
time and place stated below in order to elect officers and transact such other business as may lawfully come before the meeting. We hereby waive all notice of such meeting and of any adjournment
t   h   e   r   e   o   f   .

Place of Meeting:_____

Date of Meeting:_____

Time of Meeting:_____

_____

_____

_____

_____

Dated:_____   _____
                                    Shareholders

MINUTES, FIRST MEETING
OF SHAREHOLDERS

The first meeting of the shareholders of
was held at
on the   day of   , 20   , at   . m.

The meeting was duly called to order by the President, who stated the purpose of the meet-
i   n   g   .

Next, the Secretary read the list of shareholders as they appear in the record book of the Corporation and reported the presence of a quorum of shareholders.

Next, the Secretary read a waiver of notice of the meeting, signed by all shareholders. On a motion duly made, seconded and carried, the waiver was ordered appended to the minutes of this meet-
i   n   g   .

Next, the President asked the Secretary to read:

(1) the minutes of the organization meeting of the Corporation; and
(2) the minutes of the first meeting of the Board of Directors.

A motion was duly made, seconded and carried unanimously that the following resolution be adopted:

WHEREAS, the minutes of the organization meeting of the Corporation and the minutes of the first meeting of the Board of Directors have been read to this meeting, and

WHEREAS, bylaws were adopted and directors and officers were elected at the organization meeting, it is hereby

RESOLVED that this meeting approves and ratifies the election of the said directors and officers of this Corporation for the term of   years, and approves, ratifies and adopts said bylaws as the bylaws of the corporation. It is further

RESOLVED that all acts taken and decisions made at the organization meeting and the first meeting of the Board are approved and ratified. It is further

RESOLVED that signing of these minutes constitutes full ratification by the signatories and waiver of notice of the meeting.

There being no further business, the meeting was adjourned.

Dated the   day of   , 20   .

_____
Secretary

_____   _____
Director   Director

_____   _____
Director   Director

Appended hereto: Waiver of notice of meeting.

MINUTES, SHAREHOLDERS' ANNUAL MEETING

The Annual Meeting of Shareholders of

was held at   Province of
on the   day of   , 20   , at   o'clock,   .m.

The President duly called the meeting to order and outlined its purposes.

The Secretary next stated that a notice of meeting had been properly served, introducing an affidavit to this effect which was ordered placed on file. (OR: The Secretary stated that a waiver of notice of the meeting had been properly signed by the shareholders and it was placed on file.)

The President proposed the immediate election of a Chairman. A motion to that effect was duly made and carried.

It being determined that a quorum was present either in person or by proxy, a voice vote of shareholders was taken.   was elected Chairman of the meeting.

A motion was duly made and carried that the Secretary read the minutes of the preceding meeting of shareholders. Upon completion of the reading, a motion was duly made and carried that the minutes be approved as read.   (OR: A motion was duly made and carried that a reading of the preceding meeting of shareholders be waived.)

The President then presented his/her annual report. (Include report.)

A motion was duly made, seconded and carried that the report be received and filed.

The Secretary next presented his/her report. (Include report.)

A motion was duly made, seconded and carried that the report be received and filed.

The Treasurer then presented his/her report. (Include report.)

A motion was duly made, seconded and carried that the report be received and filed.

The Chairman said that election of directors of the Corporation for the coming year was the next order of business.

The following were nominated as directors:

The Chairman then stated that the Board has appointed   and
                                   as inspectors of election and that they would receive and tally the ballots.

160

Each shareholder was asked to place his vote in a ballot, stating the number of shares voted, and to sign his name.

The inspectors, after completing a tally of the vote, declared that the following votes had been cast:

Names of Nominees   Number of Votes

The Chairman then announced that the following persons had been elected directors:

A motion was duly made, seconded and carried that the inspectors file the report with the Clerk of Province (when required by law) and the the Secretary of the Corporation.

There being no further business, a motion was duly made, seconded and carried that the meeting be adjourned.

Dated the   day of   , 20   .

_____
Secretary

NOTICE TO DIRECTORS
OF REGULAR BOARD MEETING

A meeting of the Board of   will   be

held at the office of the Corporation at   ,

City of   , Province of   , on the

day of   , 20   , at   o'clock   .m., for

the purpose of transacting all such business as may properly come before the same.

Dated the   day of   , 20   .

_____
        Secretary

MINUTES, REGULAR BOARD MEETING

A meeting of the Board was held at   on the
day of   , 20   at   o'clock   .m.

The President called the meeting to order.

The Secretary called the roll. The following directors were present:

The Secretary reported that notice of the time and place of holding the meeting had been given to each director by mail in accordance with the bylaws.

A motion was duly made, seconded and carried that the notice be filed.

The President then stated that, a quorum being present, the meeting could transact business.

Minutes of the preceding meeting of the Board, held   ,

20   , were read and adopted.

The President presented his/her report.

A motion was made, seconded and carried that the President's report be filed.

A motion was made, seconded and carried, that   be appointed to audit the books of the Treasurer before the same are presented to the shareholders.

A motion was duly made and carried that the meeting elect officers for the ensuing year.

The following were thereupon elected by ballot:

President:

Vice-President:

Secretary:

Treasurer:

A motion was duly made and carried that salaries of officers be fixed as follows:

Name	Salary per year
Name	Salary per year
Name	Salary per year

There was no further business. The meeting was adjourned.

Dated: , 20   .

_____
Secretary

MINUTES, DIRECTORS' MEETING

A regular meeting of the Board of Directors of the Corporation was held at the office of the Corporation, at   , on   , (year), at   o'clock   .m.

There were present and participating at the meeting:

being a quorum of the directors of the Corporation.

                                              , President of the Corporation, acted as Chairman of the meeting, and   , Secretary of the Corporation, acted as Secretary of the meeting.

The Secretary presented notice or a waiver of notice of the meeting, signed by all the directors.

The meeting, having been duly convened, was ready to proceed with its business, whereupon it was:

RESOLVED, That the salary of   , as President of the Corporation, be fixed at   Dollars ($) per year.

RESOLVED, Further that the salary of   , as Vice President of the Corporation, be fixed at   Dollars ($) per year.

RESOLVED, Further that the salary of   , as Treasurer of the Corporation, be fixed at   Dollars ($) per year.

RESOLVED, Further that the salary of   , as Secretary of the Corporation,
be fixed at   Dollars ($) per year.

RESOLVED, That in addition to their present salaries, the officers of the Corporation,

comprising   ,   ,

                                        , and   ,

holding, respectively, the offices of   ,   ,

                                        , and   ,

shall participate in all fringe benefit programs available to employees of the Corporation from time
to time.

A True Record

Attest

_____

Chairman

_____

Secretary

ASSIGNMENT OF ASSETS

This agreement is made and entered into this _____ day of _____ , 20____ , by and between _____ (Stockholder), and _____ , a Corporation hereinafter referred to as "Corporation."

WITNESSETH:

WHEREAS, on the _____ day of _____ , 20____ , the Corporation will have been formed by Articles of Incorporation being filed with the Secretary of Province of _____ and at the time it was necessary to transfer certain assets into the Corporation in order to capitalize the Corporation; and

WHEREAS, _____ is desirous of transferring to the Corporation certain assets shown on the attached Exhibit "A", and the Corporation is desirous of receiving said assets,

NOW, THEREFORE, for and in consideration of the mutual covenants and agreements hereinafter entered into, it is agreed as follows:

1. _____ does hereby transfer and assign those assets listed on the attached Exhibit "A" to the Corporation.

2. In consideration for said transfer, the Corporation issues to _____ , _____ shares (____) of stock in the Corporation, par value $ ____ per share.

DATED this _____ day of _____ , 20____ .

_____
Stockholder

By: _____
Corporation

NOTICE TO SHAREHOLDERS
OF ANNUAL MEETING

The Annual Meeting of Shareholders of

for the purpose of electing   Directors, and transacting such other business as

may properly come before the meeting, will be held on the   day of

, 20   , at   o'clock   .m., at the office of   ,

City of   , and Province of   .

Transfer books will remain closed from the   day of   ,

20   , until the   day of   , 20   .

Dated the   day of   , 20   .

_____

Secretary

STOCK LEDGER AND TRANSFER LEDGER

NAME AND ADDRESS OF STOCKHOLDERS	DATE ISSUED	NAME OF SECURITY	CERTIFICATE NUMBER	VALUE OF SHARES	DATE TRANSFERRED	CERTIFICATES TRANSFERRED	SHARES TRANSFERRED	BALANCE OF SHARES

STOCKHOLDER'S PROXY

KNOWN ALL BY THESE PRESENTS, that

, the under-

signed, being the owner(s) of ( ) shares of Stock of ,

a Corporation, do hereby constitute and appoint

, whose address is ,

in the City of Province of , my

(our) true and lawful Attorney-In-Fact, for and in my (our) name, place and stead, to vote upon the

Stock owned by me (us), or standing in my (our) name, as my (our) PROXY at the Meeting of the

Stockholders of said Corporation, to be held at , in the City of ,

Province of on ,20 , at the

hour of o'clock .m., or such other day and time as the meeting may be thereafter held by

adjournment or otherwise according the number of votes now, or may then be entitled to be voted,

hereby granting said Attorney-In-Fact full power and authority to act for me (us) and in my (our) name

at the meeting or meetings in the transaction of such other business as may come before the meeting,

as fully as I (we) could do if personally present, with full power of substitution and revocation, here-

by ratifying and confirming all that my (our) said Attorney-In-Fact or substitute may do in my (our)

place, name and stead.

This Proxy is to continue in full force until , 20 , but may

be revoked at any time by notice thereof in writing, filed with the Secretary of the Corporation.

IN WITNESS WHEREOF, I (WE) have hereunto set my(our) hand(s) and seal this

day of , 20 .

_____   _____

SWORN before me at _____)

in the Province of _____, this)

_____ day of _____, 2_____)

)

_____)

A Commissioner for taking oaths)

in and for the Province of _____.)

FORM 1
ARTICLES OF INCORPORATION
(SECTION 6)

FORMULE 1
STATUTS CONSTITUTIFS
(ARTICLE 6)

1 - Name of corporation   Dénomination de la société

2 - The place in Canada where the registered office is to be situated   Lieu au Canada où doit être situé le siège social

3 - The classes and any maximum number of shares that the corporation is authorized to issue   Catégories et tout nombre maximal d'actions que la société est autorisée à émettre

4 - Restrictions, if any, on share transfers   Restrictions sur le transfert des actions, s'il y a lieu

5 - Number (or minimum and maximum number) of directors   Nombre (ou nombre minimal et maximal) d'administrateurs

6 - Restrictions, if any, on business the corporation may carry on   Limites imposées à l'activité commerciale de la société, s'il y a lieu

7 - Other provisions, if any   Autres dispositions, s'il y a lieu

8 - Incorporators - Fondateurs

Name(s) - Nom(s)	Address (include postal code) Adresse (inclure le code postal)	Signature

FOR DEPARTMENTAL USE ONLY - À L'USAGE DU MINISTÈRE SEULEMENT
Corporation No. - N° de la société

Filed - Déposée

IC 3419 (5/95)

170

Canada Business Corporations Act

Articles of Incorporation
FORM 1
INSTRUCTIONS

Format
Documents required to be sent to the Director pursuant to the *Canada Business Corporations Act* (CBCA) must conform to sections 5 to 10 of the *Canada Business Corporations Regulations.*

Item 1
Set out the proposed corporate name that complies with sections 10 and 12 of the Act. Articles of incorporation must be accompanied by a Canada-biased NUANS search report dated not more than ninety (90) days prior to the receipt of the articles by the Director. On request, a number name may be assigned under subsection 11(2) of the Act, without a search.

Item 2
Set out the name of the place and province within Canada where the registered office is to be situated. A specific street address is not required.

Item 3
Set out the details required by paragraph 6(1)(c) of the Act, including details of the rights, privileges, restrictions and conditions attached to each class of shares. All shares must be without nominal or par value and must comply with the provisions of Part V of the Act.

Item 4
If restrictions are to be placed on the right to transfer shares of the corporation, set out a statement to this effect and the nature of such restrictions.

Item 5
State the number of directors. If cumulative voting is permitted, the number of directors must be invariable; otherwise it is permissible to specify a minimum and maximum number of directors.

Item 6
If restrictions are to be placed on the business the corporation may carry on, set out the restrictions.

Item 7
Set out any provisions, permitted by the Act or Regulations to be set out in the by-laws of the corporation, that are to form part of the articles, including any pre-emptive rights or cumulative voting provisions.

Item 8
Each incorporator must state his or her name and residential address, and affix his or her signature. If an incorporator is a body corporate, that name shall be the name of the body corporate, the address shall be that of its registered office, and the articles shall be signed by a person authorized by the body corporate.

Other Documents
The articles must be accompanied by a Notice of Registered Office (Form 3), and a Notice of Directors (Form 6). Note that a Form 6 must be sent to the Director within fifteen (15) days of any change of the directors in accordance with subsection 113(1) of the Act.

Other Notices
If a proposed corporation is to engage in
(a) the construction or operation of a pipeline for the transmission of oil or gas as defined in the *National Energy Board Act,*
(b) the construction or operation of a commodity pipeline as defined in the *National Transportation Act, 1987,*
(c) the business of an investment company within the meaning of the *Investment Companies Act,*
the incorporator shall inform the minister of the department or agency that regulates such business.

The information you provide in this document is collected under the authority of the *Canada Business Corporations Act* and will be stored in personal information bank number CCA/P-PU-093. Personal information that you provide is protected under the provisions of the *Privacy Act.* However, public disclosure pursuant to section 266 of the *Canada Business Corporations Act* is permitted under the *Privacy Act.*

Completed documents in duplicate and fees payable to the Receiver General are to be sent to:

The Director, Canada Business Corporations Act
Journal Tower South, 9th floor
365 Laurier Ave. West,
Ottawa, Ontario K1A 0C8

Canada

Loi canadienne sur les sociétés par actions

Statuts constitutifs
FORMULE 1
INSTRUCTIONS

Présentation
Tous les documents dont l'envoi au directeur est exigé par la *Loi canadienne sur les sociétés par actions* doivent être conformes aux articles 5 à 10 du *Règlement sur les sociétés par actions de régime fédéral.*

Rubrique 1
Indiquer une dénomination sociale qui satisfait aux exigences des articles 10 et 12 de la Loi. Les statuts constitutifs doivent être accompagnés d'un rapport de recherche NUANS couvrant le Canada, dont la date remonte à quatre-vingt-dix (90) jours ou moins avant la date de réception des statuts par le directeur. Si un numéro matricule est demandé en guise de dénomination sociale, il peut être assigné, sans recherche préalable, en vertu du paragraphe 11(2) de la Loi.

Rubrique 2
Indiquer le nom de l'endroit et de la province au Canada où le siège social doit être situé. Une adresse précise n'est pas requise.

Rubrique 3
Indiquer les détails requis par l'alinéa 6(1)c) de la Loi, y compris les détails des droits, privilèges, restrictions et conditions attachés à chaque catégorie d'actions. Toutes les actions doivent être sans valeur nominale ni sans valeur au pair et doivent être conformes aux dispositions de la partie V de la Loi.

Rubrique 4
Si le droit de transfert des actions de la société doit être restreint, inclure une déclaration à cet effet et indiquer la nature de ces restrictions.

Rubrique 5
Indiquer le nombre d'administrateurs. Si un vote cumulatif est prévu, ce nombre doit être fixe; autrement, il est permis de spécifier un nombre minimal et maximal d'administrateurs.

Rubrique 6
Si des limites doivent être imposées à l'activité commerciale de la société, les indiquer.

Rubrique 7
Indiquer les dispositions que la Loi ou le règlement permet d'énoncer dans les règlements administratifs de la société et qui doivent faire partie des statuts, y compris les dispositions relatives au vote cumulatif ou aux droits de préemption.

Rubrique 8
Chaque fondateur doit donner son nom, son adresse domiciliaire et apposer sa signature. Si un fondateur est une personne morale, le nom doit être celui de la personne morale, l'adresse doit être celle de son siège social, et les statuts doivent être signés par une personne autorisée par la personne morale.

Autres documents
Les statuts doivent être accompagnés d'un avis de désignation du lieu du siège social (formule 3) et d'une liste des administrateurs (formule 6). Une formule 6 doit être envoyée au directeur dans les quinze (15) jours suivant tout changement dans la composition du conseil d'administration conformément au paragraphe 113(1) de la Loi.

Autres avis
Si la société projetée doit effectuer :
a) la construction ou l'exploitation d'un pipeline pour le transport du pétrole ou du gaz, défini dans la *Loi sur l'Office national de l'énergie,*
b) la construction ou l'exploitation d'un productoduc défini dans la *Loi de 1987 sur les transports nationaux,*
c) le commerce d'une société d'investissement au sens de la *Loi sur les sociétés d'investissement,*
les fondateurs doivent informer le ministre responsable du ministère ou l'agence qui réglemente ces entreprises.

Les renseignements que vous fournissez dans ce document sont recueillis en vertu de la *Loi canadienne sur les sociétés par actions,* et seront emmagasinés dans le fichier de renseignements personnels MCC/P-PU-093. Les renseignements personnels que vous fournissez sont protégés par les dispositions de la *Loi sur la protection des renseignements personnels.* Cependant, la divulgation au public selon les termes de l'article 266 de la *Loi canadienne sur les sociétés par actions* est permise en vertu de la *Loi sur la protection des renseignements personnels.*

Les documents remplis en double et les droits payables au receveur général doivent être envoyés au :

Directeur, Loi canadienne sur les sociétés par actions
Édifice Journal tour sud, 9ième étage
365 ave Laurier ouest,
Ottawa (Ontario) K1A 0C8

 Industry Canada   Industrie Canada

Canada Business   Loi canadienne sur les
Corporations Act   sociétés par actions

FORM 6
NOTICE OF DIRECTORS
OR NOTICE OF CHANGE
OF DIRECTORS
(SECTIONS 106 AND 113)

FORMULE 6
LISTE DES ADMINISTRATEURS
OU AVIS DE CHANGEMENT
DES ADMINISTRATEURS
(ARTICLES 106 ET 113)

1 - Name of corporation - Dénomination de la société	2 - Corporation No. - N° de la société

3 - The following persons became directors of this corporation — Les personnes suivantes sont devenues administrateurs de la présente société

Name Nom	Effective Date Date d'entrée en vigueur :	Residential Address - Adresse domciliaire	Resident Canadian - Y/N Résident canadien - O/N

4 - The following persons ceased to be directors of this corporation — Les personnes suivantes ont cessé d'être administrateurs de la présente société

Name Nom	Effective Date Date d'entrée en vigueur :	Residential Address - Adresse domcilliaire

5 - The directors of this corporation now are — Les administrateurs de la présente société sont maintenant

Name - Nom	Residential Address - Adresse domciliaire	Resident Canadian - Y/N Résident canadien - O/N

Date	Signature	Title - Titre

IC 3103 (2/96)

Filed - Déposée

Canada Business Corporations Act

Notice of Directors or
Notice of Change of Directors
FORM 6
INSTRUCTIONS

Format
Documents required to be sent to the Director must be in a clear and legible form.
Complete items 1 and 5 for new corporations.
Complete items 1 through 5 for changes.

Item 1
Set out the full legal name of the corporation.

Item 2
Always set out the corporation number when filing a Notice of Change of Directors (Form 6).

Item 3, 4 and 5
With respect to each director,
(a) set out first given name, initial and family name;
(b) set out full residential address (not business address), including postal code;
(c) specify occupation clearly - e.g. manager, geologist, lawyer; and
(d) refer to the definition of "resident Canadian" in the *Canada Business Corporations Act* and *Canada Business Corporations Regulations*.

Signature
A director or authorized officer of the Corporation shall sign the Notice. If a new corporation, an incorporator shall sign the Notice.

Completed document is to be sent to:

The Director, Canada Business Corporations Act
Journal Tower South
9th Floor
365 Laurier Ave. West
Ottawa, Ontario
K1A 0C8

The information you provide in this document is collected under the authority of the *Canada Business Corporations Act* and will be stored in personal information bank number IC/PPU-049. Personal information that you provide is protected under the provisions of the *Privacy Act*. However, public disclosure pursuant to section 266 of the *Canada Business Corporations Act* is permitted under the *Privacy Act*.

Loi canadienne sur les sociétés par actions

Liste des administrateurs ou
Avis de changement des administrateurs
FORMULE 6
INSTRUCTIONS

Présentation
Tous les documents dont l'envoi au directeur est exigé doivent être clairs et lisibles.
Remplir les rubriques 1 et 5 pour les nouvelles sociétés.
Remplir les rubriques 1 à 5 si des changements sont survenus.

Rubrique 1
Indiquer la dénomination officielle complète de la société.

Rubrique 2
Iindiquer toujours le numéro de la société lors de l'envoi d'un avis de changement des administrateurs (Formule 6).

Rubrique 3, 4 et 5
En ce qui concerne chaque administrateur :
a) indiquer son prénom, ses initiales et son nom de famille;
b) donner l'adresse complète de son domicile (non son adresse d'affaires) en incluant le code postal;
c) spécifier clairement son occupation - par exemple, gérant, géologue, avocat;
d) consulter la définition de "résident canadien" dans la *Loi et le Règlement sur les sociétés par actions de régime fédéral*.

Signature
Un administrateur ou un dirigeant autorisé de la société doit signer l'avis. S'il s'agit d'une nouvelle société, un fondateur doit signer l'avis.

Le document rempli doit être envoyé au :

Directeur, Loi canadienne sur les sociétés par actions
Édifice Journal tour sud
9ième étage
365 ave Laurier ouest
Ottawa (Ontario)
K1A 0C8

Les renseignements que vous fournissez dans ce document sont recueillis en vertu de la Loi canadienne sur les sociétés par actions et seront emmagasinés dans le fichier de renseignements personnels IC/PPU-049. Les renseignements personnels que vous fournissez sont protégés par les dispositions de la *Loi sur la protection des renseignements personnels*. Cependant, la divulgation au public selon les termes de l'article 266 de la Loi canadienne sur les sociétés par actions est permise en vertu de la Loi sur la protection des renseignements personnels.

Canadä

FORM 3
NOTICE OF REGISTERED OFFICE OR
NOTICE OF CHANGE OF ADDRESS OF REGISTERED OFFICE
(SECTION 19)

FORMULE 3
AVIS DE DÉSIGNATION OU
DE CHANGEMENT D'ADRESSE DU SIÈGE SOCIAL
(ARTICLE 19)

1 | Name of the Corporation - Dénomination sociale de la société

2 | Corporation No. - N° de la société

3 | Place in Canada where the registered office is situated. (Describe the place in terms of a broad municipal definition. This place must match the place listed in Item 2 of the Articles.)

Lieu du siège social au Canada. (Indiquer le lieu selon la définition générale de municipalité. Il doit correspondre au lieu indiqué à l'article 2 des statuts.)

4 | Address of Registered Office - Adresse du siège social

CAUTION: Address of registered office must be within the place that is described in the Articles and Item 3; otherwise an amendment to the Articles is required (paragraph 173(1)(b) of the Act, use Form 4) in addition to this form.

AVIS : L'adresse du siège social doit se trouver dans les limites du lieu indiqué dans les statuts et à la rubrique 3. Sinon, il faut modifier les statuts (alinéa 173(1) b) de la Loi) et remplir, outre la présente formule, la formule 4.

5 | Effective Date of Change - Date de prise d'effet

6 | Previous Address of Registered Office - Ancienne adresse du siège social

Date	Signature	Title - Titre

For Departmental Use Only - À l'usage du ministère seulement | IC 3420 (1998/04)

Filed
Déposée ▶

Canada

174

Canada Business Corporations Act

Notice of Registered Office or
Notice of Change of Registered Office
FORM 3
INSTRUCTIONS

Format
Documents required to be sent to the Director must be in a clear and legible form.

Complete Items 1, 3 and 4 for new corporations.
Complete Items 1 to 6 for changes. Note: Where required by the Act, the changes being reported by the filing of this Form must be authorized by the director(s).

Item 1
The full legal name of the corporation.

Item 2
Complete only in the case of change of registered office.

Item 3
Set out the place in Canada where the registered office is situated as indicated in the Articles of the corporation. The description should be in terms of a broad municipal definition, not a specific street address (e.g. Montreal Urban Community, in the Province of Quebec).

Item 4
The full address at which the registered office is to be situated or to which it is to be changed.

Item 5
The date when the change of registered office is to take effect.

Item 6
The previous address of the registered office, if any.

Signature
A director or authorized officer of the corporation shall sign the Notice. If a new corporation, an incorporator shall sign the Notice.

Completed document is to be sent to:

The Director, Canada Business Corporations Act
Jean Edmonds Towers, South
9th Floor
365 Laurier Ave. West
Ottawa, Ontario
K1A 0C8

Loi canadienne sur les sociétés par actions

Avis de désignation ou
de changement du siège social
FORMULE 3
INSTRUCTIONS

Présentation
Tous les documents dont l'envoi au directeur est exigé doivent être clairs et lisibles.

Remplir les rubriques 1, 3 et 4 pour les nouvelles sociétés. Remplir les rubriques 1 à 6 si des changements sont survenus. Nota : Lorsqu'exigé par la Loi, les changements rapportés par le dépôt de cette formule doivent être autorisés par les administrateurs.

Rubrique 1
La dénomination sociale complète de la société.

Rubrique 2
À remplir seulement dans le cas d'un avis de changement du siège social.

Rubrique 3
Indiquer le lieu au Canada où se situe le siège social, tel qu'il est indiqué dans les statuts de la société. Il s'agit de décrire le lieu en général, en fonction de la municipalité plutôt que par rapport à une adresse municipale précise (ex. dans la Communauté urbaine de Montréal, province de Québec).

Rubrique 4
L'adresse complète du siège social ou celle où il doit désormais être situé.

Rubrique 5
La date à laquelle le changement du siège social doit prendre effet.

Rubrique 6
L'adresse précédente du siège social, le cas échéant.

Signature
Un administrateur ou un dirigeant autorisé de la société doit signer l'avis. S'il s'agit d'une nouvelle société, un fondateur doit signer l'avis.

Le document rempli doit être envoyé au :

Directeur, Loi canadienne sur les sociétés par actions
Tours Jean-Edmonds, sud
9ième étage
365, av. Laurier ouest
Ottawa (Ontario)
K1A 0C8

BRITISH COLUMBIA

**Ministry of Finance
and Corporate Relations**
Corporate and Personal
Property Registries

Additional information and forms are available on the internet at:
http://www.fin.gov.bc.ca/registries/default.htm

Mailing Address:
PO Box 9431 Stn Prov Govt
Victoria BC   V8W 9V3

Location:
2nd Floor – 940 Blanshard
Street
Victoria BC

**Enquiries:
(250) 356-8648**

**STATEMENT ON REGISTRATION
EXTRAPROVINCIAL COMPANY**

(Section 299 *Company Act*) FORM 13

1. Full name of corporation

2. Date of incorporation or amalgamation

| YYYY | MM | DD |

3. Current jurisdiction of incorporation

4. Describe the business that the corporation will carry on in British Columbia – *State briefly, do not describe all the objects of the corporation*

5. Address of the head office **outside** British Columbia

FULL ADDRESS (INCLUDE POSTAL/ZIP CODE)

6. Complete physical address of the head office **within** British Columbia – *See Instructions in Box C*

ADDRESS	CITY	PROV.	POSTAL CODE
		B. C.	

7. Full name of the B.C. resident appointed by the corporation as its attorney for service under part 10 of the *Company Act;*

LAST NAME	FIRST NAME AND INITIALS (IF ANY)

COMPLETE PHYSICAL ADDRESS OF THE B.C. RESIDENT ATTORNEY – *SEE INSTRUCTIONS*	CITY	PROV.	POSTAL CODE
		B. C.	

OR, If attorney is a corporation, state corporation name in full as well as a complete registered office address in B.C.

CORPORATE NAME

REGISTERED OFFICE ADDRESS	CITY	PROV.	POSTAL CODE
		B. C.	

8. List the charter documents of the corporation – *Attach copies, verified by a Notary or by the proper authority in the corporation's current jurisdiction. Please refer to instructions for definition and requirements for verifying charter documents.*

DATE			DOCUMENT	DATE			DOCUMENT
YYYY	MM	DD		YYYY	MM	DD	

FIN 752 Rev. 2000 / 11 / 17

9. Full names and addresses of all **directors** of the corporation. (Attach an additional sheet if more space is required)

LAST NAME	FIRST NAME AND INITIALS (IF ANY)	FULL ADDRESS (INCLUDE POSTAL/ZIP CODE)

10. Full names and addresses of all **officers** of the corporation. (Attach an additional sheet if more space is required)

LAST NAME	FIRST NAME AND INITIALS (IF ANY)	OFFICE HELD	FULL ADDRESS (INCLUDE POSTAL/ZIP CODE)

11. Does the corporation intend to offer any of its securities to any person in British Columbia? ☐ YES ☐ NO

12. Do the directors and officers of the corporation qualify under Section 114 and 133 of the *Company Act* to become or act as directors and officers of a company incorporated under the *Company Act*? (In the instructions, Box E sets out Section 114 and Box F sets out Section 133 of the *Company Act*) ☐ YES ☐ NO (If NO, supply name and reason on attachment)

AUTHORIZED SIGNING OFFICER'S NAME (PLEASE PRINT)	SIGNATURE	RELATIONSHIP TO CORPORATION	DATE SIGNED
	X		YYYY MM DD

CONSENT – I hereby consent to act as the attorney of the above mentioned corporation.

NAME OF ATTORNEY	CITY

ATTORNEY SIGNATURE, OR AUTHORIZED SIGNING OFFICER IF ATTORNEY IS A CORPORATION	DATE SIGNED
X	YYYY MM DD

WITNESS NAME (TO THE ATTORNEY'S SIGNATURE)	WITNESS SIGNATURE
	X

ADDRESS OF WITNESS	DATE SIGNED
	YYYY MM DD

FIN 752 Rev. 2000 / 11 / 17

 **BRITISH COLUMBIA**

Ministry of Finance and Corporate Relations
Corporate and Personal Property Registries

Mailing Address:
PO Box 9431 Stn Prov Govt
Victoria BC V8W 9V3
Location:
2nd Floor – 940 Blanshard Street
Victoria BC

NOTICE OF DIRECTORS
Form 8 / 9
Sections 113 and 132 *COMPANY ACT*

Telephone: (250) 356-8626
Hours: 8:30 – 4:30 (Monday – Friday)

INSTRUCTIONS:

1. **Please type or print clearly in block letters and ensure that the form is signed and dated in ink. Complete all areas of the form. The Registry may have to return documents that do not meet this standard. Attach an additional sheet if more space is required.**
2. In Box A, enter the exact name of the company as shown on the Certificate of Incorporation, Amalgamation, Continuation or Change of Name.
3. In Box D, E and F, enter the last name, first name, and any initials of the company's directors as indicated.
4. In Box F, the residential address of a director must be a complete **physical address**. You may include general delivery, post office box, rural route, site or comp. number as part of the address, but the Registry can not accept this information as a complete address. You must also include a postal code. If an area does not have street names or numbers, provide a description that would readily allow a person to locate the director.
5. If changes occurred on more than one date, you must complete a separate Notice of Directors form for each date.
6. An individual who has ceased being a director cannot sign this form.
7. **Filing fee: $20.00.** Submit this form with a cheque or money order payable to the Minister of Finance and Corporate Relations, or provide the Registry authorization to debit the fee from a BC Online Deposit Account.
8. Additional information and forms are available on the internet at: http://www.fin.gov.bc.ca/registries

B CERTIFICATE OF INCORPORATION NO.

OFFICE USE ONLY – DO NOT WRITE IN THIS AREA

Freedom of Information and Protection of Privacy Act (FIPPA): The personal information requested on this form is made available to the public under the authority of the *Company Act*. Questions about how the *FIPPA* applies to this personal information can be directed to the Administrative Analyst, Corporate and Personal Property Registries at (250) 356-0944, PO Box 9431 Stn Prov Govt, Victoria BC   V8W 9V3.

A FULL NAME OF COMPANY

C DATE OF CHANGE
YYYY   MM   DD

D Full names of new directors **appointed:**

LAST NAME	FIRST NAME AND INITIALS *(IF ANY)*

E Full names of persons who have **ceased** to be directors:

LAST NAME	FIRST NAME AND INITIALS *(IF ANY)*

F Full names and addresses of **all** the directors of the company **as at the date of change listed above:**

LAST NAME	FIRST NAME AND INITIALS *(IF ANY)*	RESIDENTIAL ADDRESS *(INCLUDE POSTAL/ZIP CODE)*

G **CERTIFIED CORRECT** – I have read this form and found it to be correct.
Signature of a current Director, Officer, or Company Solicitor

DATE SIGNED
YYYY   MM   DD

X _____

FIN 753 Rev. 2001 / 1 / 12 (Prescribed)

 **BRITISH COLUMBIA**

**Ministry of Finance
And Corporate Relations**
Corporate and Personal
Property Registries

Mailing Address:
PO Box 9431 Stn Prov Govt
Victoria BC V8W 9V3
Location:
2nd Floor – 940 Blanshard Street
Victoria BC

**NOTICE OF OFFICES
Form 3**
Section 8 *COMPANY ACT*

Telephone: (250) 356-8648
Hours: 8:30 – 4:30 (Monday – Friday)

A **FULL NAME OF COMPANY** – Please show the exact name as stated in the memorandum of the company

OFFICE USE ONLY – DO NOT WRITE IN THIS AREA

INSTRUCTIONS

1. **Please type or print clearly in block letters and ensure that the form is signed and dated in ink. Complete all areas of the form. The Registry may have to return documents that do not meet this standard.**

2. In Box B and C, enter the complete physical address of the office. You may include general delivery, post office box, rural route, site or comp. number as part of the address, but the Registry can not accept this information as a complete address. You must also include a postal code. If an area does not have street names or numbers, provide a description that would readily allow a person to locate the office.

Freedom of Information and Protection of Privacy Act
The personal information requested on this form is made available to the public under the authority of the Company Act. Questions about the collection or use of this information can be directed to the Administrative Analyst, Corporate and Personal Property Registries at (250) 356-0944, PO Box 9431 Stn Prov Gov't, Victoria BC V8W 9V3.

B **REGISTERED OFFICE ADDRESS**

PROVINCE	POSTAL CODE
B.C.	

C **RECORDS OFFICE ADDRESS**

PROVINCE	POSTAL CODE
B.C.	

D **SIGNATURE OF SUBSCRIBER/SOLICITOR** – I have read this form and found it to be correct.

DATE SIGNED
YYYY   MM   DD

FIN 720 Rev. 1999 / 3 / 10 (Prescribed)

MANITOBA

The Corporations Act/
Loi sur les corporations
ARTICLES OF INCORPORATION (share capital)
STATUTS CONSTITUTIFS (avec capital-actions)

Corporation No.
Nᵒ de la corporation

1—Name of Corporation / Dénomination sociale

2—The address in full of the registered office (include postal code) /
Adresse complète du bureau enregistré (inclure le code postal)

3—Number (or minimum and maximum number) of directors /
Nombre (ou nombre minimal et maximal) d'administrateurs

4—First directors / Premiers administrateurs

Name in full / Nom complet	Address in full (include postal code) / Adresse complète (inclure le code postal)

5—The classes and any maximum number of shares that the corporation is authorized to issue /
Catégories et tout nombre maximal d'actions que la corporation est autorisée à émettre

6—The rights, privileges, restrictions and conditions attaching to the shares, if any /
   Droits, privilèges, restrictions et conditions dont les actions sont assorties, s'il y a lieu

7—Restrictions, if any, on share transfers / Restrictions au transfert des actions, s'il y a lieu

8—Restrictions, if any, on business the corporation may carry on /
   Limites imposées quant à l'entreprise que la corporation peut exercer, s'il y a lieu

9—Other provisions, if any / Autres dispositions, s'il y a lieu

10—I have satisfied myself that, the proposed name of the corporation is not the same as or similar to the name of any known body corporate, association, partnership, individual or business so as to be likely to confuse or mislead. /
   Je me suis assuré que la dénomination sociale projetée n'est ni identique ni semblable à la dénomination d'une personne morale, d'une association, d'une société ou d'une entreprise connue ou au nom d'un particulier connu et qu'elle ne saurait prêter à confusion ni induire en erreur.

11—Incorporators / Fondateurs

Name in full / Nom complet	Address in full (include postal code) / Adresse complète (inclure le code postal)	Signature / Signature

Note: If any First Director named in paragraph 4 is not an Incorporator, a Form 3 "Consent to Act as a First Director" must be attached. State the full civic address in paragraphs 2, 4 and 11—a P.O. box number alone is not acceptable. /

Remarque : Si l'un des premiers administrateurs nommés à la rubrique 4 n'est pas un fondateur, joindre la formule 3 intitulée "Consentement à agir en qualité de premier administrateur". Indiquer l'adresse complète dans les rubriques 2, 4 et 11; un numéro de case postale seul n'est pas suffisant.

The Corporations Act /
Loi sur les corporations

REQUEST FOR CORPORATE NAME RESERVATION
DEMANDE DE RÉSERVATION D'UNE DÉNOMINATION SOCIALE

Manitoba

CAUTION : RESPONSIBILITY FOR CHOICE AND USE OF THE NAME RESTS ENTIRELY WITH THE APPLICANT. READ GUIDELINES ON REVERSE BEFORE ANSWERING ALL QUESTIONS.
ATTENTION: LE CHOIX ET L'UTILISATION DE LA DÉNOMINATION INCOMBENT AU REQUÉRANT. LIRE LES DIRECTIVES QUI FIGURENT AU VERSO AVANT DE RÉPONDRE AUX QUESTIONS

A Name and address of sender / Nom et adresse de l'expéditeur

Contact person / Personne ressource

Tel (8:30-4:30) / Tél(8 h 30-16 h 30) :

B 1. Proposed name / Dénomination projetée

2. Reason for reservation / Motif de la réservation

☐ INCORPORATION / CONSTITUTION EN CORPORATION
☐ AMALGAMATION / FUSION
☐ REGISTRATION OF FEDERAL CORPORATION / ENREGISTREMENT D'UNE CORPORATION FÉDÉRALE
☐ REGISTRATION OF EXTRA- PROVINCIAL CORPORATION / ENREGISTREMENT D'UNE CORPORATION EXTRA-PROVINCIALE
☐ TRUST AND LOAN CORPORATION / CORPORATIONS DE FIDUCIE ET CORPORATIONS DE PRÊT
☐ REVIVAL OR RESTORATION / RECONSTITUTION OU RÉTABLISSEMENT
☐ CONTINUANCE / PROROGATION
☐ CHANGE OF NAME FROM / CHANGEMENT DE DÉNOMINATION DE _____

CURRENT NAME / DÉNOMINATION ACTUELLE

3. Describe the main type of business to be carried on in Manitoba / Indiquer l'entreprise principale qui sera poursuivie

4. How or why name was chosen / Indiquer les raisons du choix de la dénomination

5. Note any relevant information (e.g.names of affiliated businesses, consents available from other companies, etc)
Donner tout autre renseignement pertinent (e.g. le nom des entreprises qui appartiennent au même groupe, le consentement d'autres compagnies, etc.)

C **OFFICE REPLY / RÉPONSE**

☐ **YES,** the name appears to be available and is reserved for you for **90 DAYS** until
OUI, la dénomination semble disponible et elle est réservée pour **90 JOURS** jusqu'au

☐ **NO,** the name is not available. Please see reasons on reverse.
NON, la dénomination n'est pas disponible pour les motifs indiqués au verso.

REMARKS / REMARQUES _____

DATE/DATE	SIGNATURE/ SIGNATURE	TEL/ TÉL
		945-

MG10234 (REV 04/92)   FORM 25/ FORMULE 25

COMPANIES OFFICE
1010 - 405 BROADWAY
WINNIPEG, MANITOBA, R3C 3L6
(204) 945 - 2500

OFFICE DES COMPAGNIES
405, BROADWAY, BUREAU 1010
WINNIPEG (MANITOBA) R3C 3L6
(204) 945 -2500

GUIDELINES

1. A corporate name reservation request will result in a four page report. The first two pages list names on record in Manitoba. The last two pages will list some trademarks and names in use in other Canadian jurisdictions. It is your responsibility to ensure that the name you choose is not identical or confusingly similar to an existing trademark, business, association or corporation. If anyone complains about your name, and that complaint is held to be valid, it will be your obligation to change your name.

2.You can check for similar names by reading telephone directories, trade publications, magazines, advertisements, and by contacting the corporations branches in other jurisdictions.

3. Reservation of a name is not "protection" or a "guarantee" that your name is automatically available. Use of a name is done at the risk of the user.

4. If the name is not available, a new name must be selected, AND a new Reservation form AND FEE will have to be filed. Careful selection and research of a name may save you time and money.

5. Read the reasons for rejection listed below. These may help in choosing a name.

DIRECTIVES

1. Un rapport de quatre pages vous sera remis après le dépôt de votre demande de réservation d'une dénomination sociale. Les deux premières pages donnent les dénominations enregistrées au Manitoba. Les autres pages donnent certaines marques de commerce et dénominations utilisées ailleurs au Canada. Il vous incombe de veiller à ce que la dénomination choisie ne soit pas identique à une marque de commerce ou à une dénomination existante et qu'elle ne prête pas à confusion avec une telle marque de commerce ou dénomination. Si quelqu'un portait plainte au sujet de votre dénomination et que cette plainte s'avérait fondée, vous devriez alors changer de dénomination.

2.Vous pouvez vérifier s'il existe des dénominations semblables en consultant les annuaires téléphoniques, les publications commerciales, les périodiques, les annonces et en communiquant avec la direction des corporations d'autres administrations.

3. La réservation d'une dénomination ne vous garantit pas que votre dénomination sera automatiquement retenue. L'utilisation de la dénomination se fait au risque de l'utilisateur.

4.Si la dénomination ne peut être retenue, vous devez en choisir une autre et déposer une nouvelle formule de réservation accompagnée du droit prescrit. Vous épargnerez temps et argent en choisissant avec soin votre dénomination.

5. Lisez les motifs de rejet ci-dessous. Cela facilitera le choix d'une dénomination.

REASONS FOR REJECTION OF NAME / MOTIFS DE REJET DE LA DÉNOMINATION

☐ Prohibited / Dénomination interdite.

☐ Consists of general words **or** only describes the nature of business./
Dénomination entièrement formée de termes généraux **ou** ne faisant que décrire la nature de l'entreprise.

☐ Consists of surname or geographical name only /
Dénomination formée uniquement d'un nom de famille ou d'un toponyme.

☐ Too similar to name(s) on attached report /
Dénomination trop semblable à une ou plusieurs des dénominations figurant dans le rapport ci-joint

☐ Obscene or on public grounds objectionable /
Dénomination obscène ou inadmissible pour des raisons d'ordre public.

☐ Distinctive element should be added / Il manque un élément distinctif

☐ Descriptive element should be added / Il manque un élément descriptif

☐ Read remarks on front / Lire les remarques au recto

The Corporations Act /
Loi sur les corporations
REQUEST FOR SERVICE
DEMANDE DE SERVICE

Manitoba

A Name and address of sender / Nom et adresse de l'expéditeur   Contact person / Personne ressource

_____   _____

_____

_____   Tel(8:30-4:30) / /Tél.(8 h 30-16 h 30) _____

Fee enclosed / Droit inclus $

B Current name of the corporation/ Dénomination de la corporation

_____

Corporation number / Numéro de la corporation

C IF YOU ARE FILING ARTICLES OR AN APPLICATION, PLEASE IDENTIFY THE FORM BEING FILED /
EN CAS DE DÉPÔT DE STATUTS OU D'UNE DEMANDE, INDIQUER LA FORMULE DÉPOSÉE :

☐ Articles of incorporation / Statuts constitutifs

☐ Articles of / Statuts (Clauses) _____

☐ Application for registration / Demande d'enregistrement

☐ Application for supplementary registration / Demande d'enregistrement supplémentaire

☐ Other / Autre _____

D IF YOU WANT CERTIFICATES AND/OR COPIES, PLEASE IDENTIFY THE DESIRED ITEM (S) /
POUR OBTENIR DES CERTIFICATS OU DES PHOTOCOPIES, PRIÈRE D'INDIQUER LES DOCUMENTS DÉSIRÉS

☐ Certificate of status / Certificat de statut

☐ Certificate of search / Certificat de recherche

☐ Photocopy of / Photocopie de _____

☐ Certified copy of / Copie certifiée conforme de _____

E OFFICE REPLY / RÉPONSE

☐ Forms accepted, your copy enclosed.
Les formules sont acceptées, votre copie est jointe aux présentes

☐ Requested item(s) enclosed / Les documents demandés sont joints aux présentes

☐ REMARKS / REMARQUES _____

_____

_____

SIGNATURE FOR RECEIPT / ACCUSÉ DE RÉCEPTION (SIGNATURE)

RETURN FEE AND TWO COPIES OF FORM TO :
COMPANIES OFFICE
1010-405 BROADWAY
WINNIPEG, MANITOBA R3C 3L6

(204) 945-2500
MG10235 (REV.SEP/92)

ENVOYER LE DROIT ET DEUX COPIES DE LA FORMULE À
OFFICE DES COMPAGNIES
405, BROADWAY, BUREAU 1010
WINNIPEG (MANITOBA) R3C 3L6

(204) 945-2500
FORM 19 /FORMULE 19

<table>
<tr><td>

NEW BRUNSWICK
BUSINESS CORPORATIONS ACT
FORM 26
STATEMENT OF REGISTRATION
EXTRA-PROVINCIAL CORPORATION
(SECTION 197)

</td><td>

New Nouveau
Brunswick

</td><td>

NOUVEAU-BRUNSWICK
LOI SUR LES CORPORATIONS COMMERCIALES
FORMULE 26
DECLARATION D'ENREGISTREMENT
CORPORATION EXTRAPROVINCIALE
(ARTICLE 197)

</td></tr>
</table>

1. Name of Extra-Provincial Corporation / Nom de la corporation extraprovinciale

2. Jurisdiction of Incorporation / Juridiction de constitution

3. Date of Incorporation / Date de constitution

4. Address of Registered Office / Adresse du bureau enregistré

5. Mailing Address (if applicable) / Adresse postale (le cas échéant)

6. The place in New Brunswick where the principal office is to be situated / Emplacement du bureau principal au Nouveau-Brunswick

7. Description of business / Description des affaires au Nouveau-Brunswick

8. Names and addresses of directors / Noms et adresses des administrateurs

9. The extra-provincial corporation is a valid and subsisting corporation and has capacity to carry on business in New Brunswick and has appointed an attorney for service in New Brunswick.

9. La corporation extraprovinciale est une corporation valide et actuelle; elle est habilitée à exercer ses activités au Nouveau-Brunswick et à nommer son procureur pour fin de signification au Nouveau-Brunswick.

Date _____ 19 _____   Signature _____

Position in the Corporation
Fonction dans la corporation _____

<table>
<tr><td>

FOR DEPARTMENTAL USE ONLY

Extra Provincial Corporation No.
N° Corporation extraprovinciale

</td><td>

RÉSERVÉ AU SEUL USAGE DU MINISTÈRE

Filed
Déposé

</td></tr>
</table>

45-3653 (02/89)

BUSINESS CORPORATIONS ACT

STATEMENT OF REGISTRATION EXTRA-PROVINCIAL CORPORATION FORM 26 INSTRUCTIONS

Format

Documents required to be sent to the Director pursuant to the *Business Corporations Act* must conform to sections 4 to 9 of this Regulation.

Item 1

Set out a proposed corporate name and any business name registered under the Partnerships and Business Names Act which is required in order to comply with section 199 of the Act.

Item 2

State the jurisdiction where the extra-provincial corporation was incorporated.

Item 4

Registered office means the head office or principal office outside of New Brunswick.

Item 6

Set out the name of the place within New Brunswick where the principal office is to be situated. If there is no office, give name and address of attorney for service.

Item 7

State the principal business being carried out in New Brunswick.

Other documents

This statement must be accompanied by a certificate of incorporation which should state the current status of the extra-provincial corporation, the appointment of the attorney for service in Form 25 and the fee. For Items 4, 5, 6 and 8, set out the full address giving the street number or R.R. number, municipality or Post Office, province and postal code. P.O. Box is not sufficient. Note that a Form 29 must be sent to the Director within 30 days of any change of directors in accordance with subsection 206(1) and a Form 25 if there has been a change of attorney for service in accordance with subsection 203(1).

The fee for registration is $200 which is payable by cheque to the Minister of Finance.

The cost for the publication of the notice of the registration in The Royal Gazette is $10.00 which is payable by cheque to the Minister of Finance.

Signature

A director or authorized officer of the extra-provincial corporation shall sign the statement.

Completed documents in duplicate and fees payable to the Minister of Finance are to be sent to:

> The Director, Corporations Branch
> Corporate & Trust Affairs
> Department of Justice
> P.O. Box 6000, Fredericton, N.B.
> E3B 5H1

45-3653 (02/89)

LOI SUR LES CORPORATIONS COMMERCIALES

DECLARATIONS D'ENREGISTREMENT CORPORATION EXTRAPROVINCIALE FORMULE 26 INSTRUCTIONS

Format

Les documents dont l'envoi au Directeur est requis en application de la *Loi sur les corporations commerciales* doivent être conformes aux articles 4 à 9 du présent règlement.

Article 1

Indiquer la raison sociale proposée et toute appellation commerciale enregistrées en application de la Loi sur l'enregistrement des sociétés en nom collectif et des appellations commerciales; cette formalité est requise afin de permettre à la corporation d'être conforme à l'article 199 de la Loi.

Article 2

Déclarer la juridiction de constitution de la corporation extraprovinciale.

Article 4

Bureau enregistré désigne le siège social ou le bureau principal situé à l'extérieur du Nouveau-Brunswick.

Article 6

Indiquer le nom de la localité à l'intérieur du Nouveau-Brunswick où se trouve le bureau principal. A défaut de bureau, donner le nom et l'adresse du procureur pour fin de signification.

Article 7

Déclarer l'activité principale de la corporation au Nouveau-Brunswick.

Autres documents

Cette déclaration doit être accompagnée d'un certificat de constitution qui devrait indiquer le statut actuel de la corporation extraprovinciale, la nomination du procureur pour fin de signification selon la formule 25 et les droits. En ce qui concerne les articles 4, 5, 6 et 8, indiquer l'adresse au complet donnant le numéro de la rue ou de la R.R., la municipalité ou le bureau de poste, la province et le code postal. Le numéro de la case postale seul est insuffisant. Remarquer qu'une formule 29 doit être envoyée au Directeur dans les 30 jours de tout changement d'administrateurs conformément au paragraphe 206(1) ainsi qu'une formule 25 en cas où il y a changement du procureur pour fin de signification conformément au paragraphe 203(1).

Les droits d'enregistrement sont de $200 payables par chèque au ministre des Finances.

Les frais de publication de l'avis de l'enregistrement dans le Gazette royale sont de $10, payables par chèque au ministre des Finances.

Signature

Un administrateur ou un dirigeant autorisé de la corporation extraprovinciale doit signer l'avis.

Les documents complets, établis en double exemplaires, doivent être envoyés au:

> Directeur du service des corporations
> Affaires corporatives et fiduciaires
> Ministère de la Justice
> C.P. 6000, Fredericton, Nouveau-Brunswick
> E3B 5H1

New / Nouveau Brunswick

BUSINESS CORPORATIONS ACT FORM 1 ARTICLES OF INCORPORATION (SECTION 4)	LOI SUR LES CORPORATIONS COMMERCIALES FORMULE 1 STATUTS CONSTITUTIFS (ARTICLE 4)

1 - Name of Corporation: / Raison sociale de la corporation:

2 - The classes and any maximum number of shares that the corporation is authorized to issue and any maximum aggregate amount for which shares may be issued including shares without par value and/or with par value and the amount of the par value: / Les catégories et le nombre maximal d'actions que la corporation peut émettre ainsi que le montant maximal global pour lequel les actions peuvent être émises y compris les actions sans valeur au pair ou avec valeur au pair ou les deux et le montant de la valeur au pair:

3 - Restrictions, if any, on share transfers: / Restrictions, s'il y en a, au transfert d'actions:

4 - Number (or minimum and maximum number) of directors: / Nombre (ou nombre minimum et maximum) des administrateurs:

5 - Restrictions, if any, on business the corporation may carry on: / Restrictions, s'il y en a, à l'activité que peut exercer la corporation:

6 - Other provisions, if any: / D'autres dispositions, le cas échéant:

7 - Incorporators: / Fondateurs:

Date	Names - Noms	Address (include postal code) Adresses (y compris le code postal)	Signature

FOR DEPARTMENT USE ONLY	RÉSERVÉ À L'USAGE DU MINISTÈRE
Corporation No. - N°. de Corporation	Filed - Déposé

45-4104 (1/94)   NEWSOME AND GILBERT   784, 362-417

187

New Nouveau Brunswick

| BUSINESS CORPORATIONS ACT FORM 2 NOTICE OF REGISTERED OFFICE OR NOTICE OF CHANGE OF REGISTERED OFFICE (SECTION 17) | LOI SUR LES CORPORATIONS COMMERCIALES FORMULE 2 AVIS DE DESIGNATION OU AVIS DE CHANGEMENT DU BUREAU ENREGISTRÉ (ARTICLE 17) |

1 - Name of Corporation - Raison sociale de la corporation:

2 - Corporation No. - N°. de corporation:

3 - Place and address of the registered office:

Lieu et adresse du bureau enregistré:

4 - Effective date of change:

Date d'entrée en vigueur du changement:

5 - Previous place and address of the registered office:

Derniers lieu et adresse du bureau enregistré:

Date	Signature	Description of Office Fonction

45-4105 (1/94)   DYE & DURHAM CO. INC.   784, 362-418

New Nouveau **Brunswick**

| BUSINESS CORPORATIONS ACT
FORM 4
NOTICE OF DIRECTORS
OR NOTICE OF CHANGE OF DIRECTORS
(SECTION 64, 71) | LOI SUR LES CORPORATIONS COMMERCIALES
FORMULE 4
LISTE DES ADMINISTRATEURS OU
AVIS DE CHANGEMENT D'ADMINISTRATEURS
(ARTICLE 64, 71) |

1 - Name of Corporation: Raison sociale de la corporation:

2 - The following persons became directors of this corporation: **Liste des personnes devenues administrateurs de la corporation:**

Effective Date Date d'entrée en vigueur		D/J	M/M	Y/A			
Name / Nom			Residential Address or Address for Service Adresse résidentielle ou adresse pour fin de signification			Occupation	Telephone Téléphone

3 - The following persons ceased to be directors of this corporation: Liste des personnes qui ont cessé d'être administrateurs de la corporation:

Effective Date Date d'entrée en vigueur	D/J	M/M	Y/A
Name / Nom	Residential Address or Address for Service Adresse résidentielle ou adresse pour fin de signification		

4 - The directors of the corporation now are: Administrateurs actuels de la corporation:

Name / Nom	Residential Address or Address for Service Adresse résidentielle ou adresse pour fin de signification	Occupation	Telephone Téléphone

Date	Signature	Description of Office Fonction

| For Department Use Only / Réservé à l'usage du ministère | Form 4 / Formule 4
Filed / Déposé |

45- 4119 (10/95)

189

GOVERNMENT OF
NEWFOUNDLAND AND LABRADOR

Department of Government Services and Lands
THE CORPORATIONS ACT
FORM 24

STATEMENT FOR
REGISTRATION – EXTRA-PROVINCIAL COMPANY
(Section 438)

1. Name of Company _____

2. The company was incorporated in _____

    on the _____ day of _____ , and is at this date a valid and
    subsisting corporation, legally authorized to transact business under its charter and regulations.

3. The company was incorporated under _____

4. The business which the company will carry on in Newfoundland is _____

    _____

5. The company commenced business (or intends to commence business) in Newfoundland on the

    _____ day of _____ 19____ .

6. The charter and regulations of the company, a verified copy of which is lodged herewith, consists
    of the following documents:

    Date _____

    Nature of Document _____

7. The period fixed by its charter for the duration of the company is _____ years

    from _____

8. The liability of the members of the company under its charter is _____

9. The authorized share capital of the company is $ _____ and is divided

    into _____ shares of $ _____ each.

    The number of shares without nominal or par value authorized is _____

    The subscribed capital at the date hereof is $ _____

    The paid-up capital at the date hereof is $ _____

    The shares in the company consist of _____

10. The full address of the head office or chief place of business outside Newfoundland is _____

_____

_____

11. The full address of the head office or chief place of business in Newfoundland will be _____

_____

_____

12. The directors of the company are _____

_____

_____

_____

_____

_____

_____

13. Other information _____

IN WITNESS OF WHICH the common seal of the company was affixed on the _____

day of _____ 19 _____

The common seal of
was affixed in the
presence of
                              _____
                              Officer of the Company

                                                    Affix Seal
                                                    of Company

_____   _____
Witness sign here   *Officer of the Company*

GOVERNMENT OF
NEWFOUNDLAND AND LABRADOR

THE CORPORATIONS ACT

FORM 1

ARTICLES OF INCORPORATION

(Sections 12, 421, 463, 490)

1 – Name of Corporation

2 – The place in Newfoundland where the registered office is to be situated

3 – The classes and maximum number of shares that the corporation is authorized to issue

4 – Restrictions if any on share transfers

5 – Number (or minimum and maximum number) of directors

6 – Restrictions if any on business the corporation may carry on

7 – Other provisions if any

8 – Incorporators

Names	Address (Include Postal Code)	Signature

For Department use only

Corporation No. –

GOVERNMENT OF
NEWFOUNDLAND AND LABRADOR

THE CORPORATIONS ACT

FORM 3

NOTICE OF REGISTERED OFFICE OR
NOTICE OF CHANGE OF REGISTERED OFFICE
(Section 34)

1 - Name of corporation	2 - Corporation No.

3 - Address of the registered office (include mailing address)

4 - Effective date of change

5 - Previous address of the registered office

Date	Signature	Description of Office

Registry of Companies, P.O. Box 8700, Confederation Bldg., St. John's, NF A1B 4J6

GOVERNMENT OF
NEWFOUNDLAND AND LABRADOR

THE CORPORATIONS ACT

FORM 6

NOTICE OF DIRECTORS
(Sections 175, 183)

1 - Name of Corporation	2 - Corporation No.

3 - The following persons became directors of this corporation:
Effective Date

Name	Residential Address	Occupation

4 - The following persons ceased to be directors of this corporation:
Effective Date

Name	Residential Address

5 - The directors of this corporation now are:

Name	Residential Address	Occupation	Citizenship

Date	Signature	Description of Office

Registry of Companies, P.O. Box 8700, Confederation Bldg., St. John's, NF A1B 4J6

194

NOVA SCOTIA
Business and Consumer Services
Registry of Joint Stock Companies

Name Reservation Request

Search Type:
Please check one)

☐ Atlantic Region Search   Fee: = $40.00 + HST = $46.00

☐ Federal Search   Fee: = $50.00 + HST = $57.50

Requested Name: _____

Nature of Business: _____

Customer Information:

Applicant: _____ _____
              (First Name)   (Last Name)

Mailing Address   _____
                                  (Address)

              _____ _____ _____
                  (City or Town)   (Province)   (Postal Code)

              _____ _____
                (Telephone Number)   (Fax Number)

(E-Mail Address)

Payment Type:

☐ Cheque

☐ Money Order

☐ Visa   _____ _____ _____
                   (Account #)   (Expiry Date - mm/yy)   (Signature)

USE OF REGISTERED NAME

TAKE NOTE that a corporation/partnership is required to do business using the exact name which has been

NOVA SCOTIA
Business and Consumer Services
Registry of Joint Stock Companies

Notice of Officers and Directors for an Incorporated Company

Companies Act

(Section 98, Chapter 81, R.S.N.S. 1989)

Company: _____

(Name)

hereby gives notice that the current officer(s) and director(s) of the company are: *See Footnote

Choose one or both: Director: ☐   Officer: ☐

_____   _____
(First Name)   (Last Name)

_____
(Street and Number)

_____   _____   _____
(City or Town)   (Province)   (Postal Code)

_____   _____
(Occupation)   (Office Held if Officer)

Choose one or both: Director: ☐   Officer: ☐

_____   _____
(First Name)   (Last Name)

_____
(Street and Number)

_____   _____   _____
(City or Town)   (Province)   (Postal Code)

_____   _____
(Occupation)   (Office Held if Officer)

Choose one or both: Director: ☐   Officer ☐

_____   _____
(First Name)   (Last Name)

_____
(Street and Number)

_____   _____   _____
(City or Town)   (Province)   (Postal Code)

_____   _____
(Occupation)   (Office Held if Officer)

Date: _____
(YYYY-MM-DD)

Director or Officer   _____
of Company   (Name)

_____
(Signature)

Registry #: ▉▉▉▉▉▉▉   Date Filed: ▉▉▉▉▉▉▉

NOVA SCOTIA
Business and Consumer Services
Registry of Joint Stock Companies

Appointment of Recognized Agent

Corporations Registration Act

Partnerships and Business Names Registration Act

Societies Act

Agent: _____ _____ *See Footnote
                    (First Name)   (Last Name)

Civic Address: _____
                                          (Street and Number)

_____ N.S. _____
         (City or Town)   (Province)   (Postal Code)

Mailing Address (if other that above):

_____
                                          (Address)

_____ _____ _____
         (City or Town)   (Province)   (Postal Code)

is hereby appointed Recognized Agent of:

_____
                    (Name of Company, Partnership or Society)

pursuant to the (please check one):   ☐   Corporations Registration Act.

                                        ☐   Partnerships and Business Names Registration Act.

                                        ☐   Societies Act.

resident within Nova Scotia, service upon whom of any writ, summons, process, notice or other document shall be deemed to be sufficient upon the Company, Partnership, or Society and each member thereof and this appointment shall be and remain in force until notice in writing by the company, Partnership, or Society that he/she has ceased to be such Agent is filed with the Registry of Joint Stock Companies.

Date: _____
                    (YYYY-MM-DD)

Officer or Partner
Signing: _____
                                          (Name)

_____ **See Footnote
                                          (Signature)

*   The Agent must be an Individual, not a firm or company.
** To be signed by an Officer or Director of the Company/Society, or, if on behalf of a Partnership, by a Partner, for and on behalf of all Partners.

Registry #: ▮▮▮▮▮▮▮   Date Filed: ▮▮▮▮▮▮▮

NOVA SCOTIA
Business and Consumer Services
Registry of Joint Stock Companies

Statement of Extra-Provincial Registration

Corporations Registration Act

(Section 8)

Name of Corporation: _____
(Name)

Incorporation Date: _____
(YYYY-MM-DD)

Incorporated Under: _____ _____
(Act Governing Incorporation)   (Jurisdiction)

Head Office Address: _____
(Street and Number)

_____ _____ _____
(City or Town)   (Province)   (Postal Code)

Nature of Business: _____

Address in Nova Scotia: _____
(Street and Number)

N.S.
_____ _____ _____
(City or Town)   (Province)   (Postal Code)

Mailing Address (if other than above): _____
(Address)

_____ _____ _____
(City or Town)   (Province)   (Postal Code)

Engaged in business in N.S. since : _____
(YYYY-MM-DD)

The following information is optional. If provided it will be for Registry use only.

_____ _____
(Telephone Number)   (Fax Number)

_____
(E-Mail Address)

I hereby make oath and say that the foregoing information and the list of Officers and Directors of the Company attached are true.

Officer of Corporation: _____ | _____
(Name) | (Position Held)

SWORN TO at _____ |

in the Province of _____ |

Sworn Date: _____ | _____
(YYYY-MM-DD) | (Signature of Officer of Corporation)

Before me, _____ |
(Notary Public, Commissioner of Oaths, Barrister) |

Registry #: ▮▮▮▮▮

Date Filed: ▮▮▮▮▮

Registry of Joint Stock Companies, P.O. Box 1529, 1505 Barrington St., 9th floor, Halifax, N.S., B3J 2Y4
(902) 424-7770

http://www.gov.ns.ca/bacs/rjsc/
Form CF020 Rev. 06/1997

198

STATUTORY DE CLARATION

(Subsection 28(2) of the Companies Act)

IN THE MATTER of the formation of a company to be called,

AND IN THE MATTER OF THE Companies Act:

I,   of

City or Town:

Province of Nova Scotia

Occupation:

do solemnly declare:

1.   **THAT** I have been engaged in the formation of the above named Company.

2.   **THAT** all of the requirements of the Companies Act of Nova Scotia in respect to registration and matters precedent and incidental thereto have been complied with in the formation of the said Company.

        AND I MAKE THIS SOLEMN DECLARATION conscientiously believing it to be true and knowing that it is of the same force and effect as if made under oath and by virtue of the Canada Evidence Act.

DECLARED before me at:

this date: (YYYY-MM-DD)

_____
(Signature)

_____
(Notary Public, Commissioner of Oaths, Barrister)

Form CF010 Rev. 07/1996

Ontario

| Ministry of Consumer and Commercial Relations | Ministère de la Consommation et du Commerce | Companies Branch 393 University Ave Suite 200 Toronto ON M5G 2M2 | Direction des compagnies 393 av. University Bureau 200 Toronto ON M5G 2M2 | Page 1/Page 1 |

FORM 2- EXTRA PROVINCIAL CORPORATIONS/
FORMULE 2 - PERSONNES MORALES EXTRA-PROVINCIALES
Please type or print all information in block capital letters using black ink.
Prière de dactylographier les renseignements ou de les écrire en caractères d'imprimerie à l'encre noire.

INITIAL RETURN/NOTICE OF CHANGE /
RAPPORT INITIAL/AVIS DE MODIFICATION
Corporations Information Act/
Loi sur les renseignements exigés des personnes morales

For Ministry Use Only / À l'usage du ministère seulement	2. Ontario Corporation Number Numéro matricule de la personne morale en Ontario	3. Date of Incorporation or Amalgamation Date de constitution, ou fusion Year/Année Month/Mois Day/Jour	1.	Initial Return Rapport initial	Notice of Change Avis de modification
			Business Corporations/ Société par actions		
			Not-For-Profit Corporation/ Personne morale sans but lucratif		

4. Corporation Name Including Punctuation/Raison sociale de la personne morale, y compris la ponctuation

For Ministry Use Only
À l'usage du ministère seulement

5. Address of Registered or Head Office/Adresse du siège social
c/o / a/s

For Ministry Use Only
À l'usage du ministère seulement

Street Number/Numéro civique   Street Name/Nom de la rue   Suite/Bureau

Street Name (cont'd)/Nom de la rue (suite)

City/Town/Ville   Province, State/Province, État

Country/Pays   Postal Code/Code postal

6. Address of Principal Office in Ontario/Adresse du bureau principal en Ontario
Street Number/Numéro civique

☐ Same as Above/ Même que celle ci-dessus   ☐ Not Applicable/ Ne s'applique pas

Street Name/Nom de la rue   Suite/Bureau

Street Name (cont'd)/Nom de la rue (suite)

City/Town/Ville

ONTARIO, CANADA

Postal Code/Code postal

7. Language of Preference Langue préférée   English/Anglais ☐   French/Français ☐

8. Former Corporation Name if applicable/Raison sociale antérieure de la personne morale, le cas échéant.

☐ Not Applicable Ne s'applique pas

9. Date commenced business activity in Ontario/ Date de début des activités en Ontario Year/Année Month/Mois Day/Jour	10. Date ceased carrying on business activity in Ontario/ Date de cessation des activités en Ontario Year/Année Month/Mois Day/Jour
	☐ Not Applicable/ Ne s'applique pas

11. Jurisdiction of Incorporation/Amalgamation or Continuation. (Check appropriate box) Do not check more than one box.
Ressort de constitution/de fusion ou prorogation (cocher la case pertinente). Ne cocher qu'une seule case.

| 1. ☐ ALBERTA ALBERTA | 2. ☐ CANADA CANADA | 3. ☐ NEW BRUNSWICK NOUVEAU-BRUNSWICK | 4. ☐ NOVA SCOTIA NOUVELLE-ÉCOSSE | 5. ☐ QUEBEC QUÉBEC | 6. ☐ YUKON YUKON | 7. ☐ BRITISH COLUMBIA COLOMBIE-BRITANNIQUE |
| 8. ☐ MANITOBA MANITOBA | 9. ☐ NEWFOUNDLAND TERRE-NEUVE | 10. ☐ PRINCE EDWARD ISLAND ÎLE-DU-PRINCE-ÉDOUARD | 11. ☐ SASKATCHEWAN SASKATCHEWAN | 12. ☐ NORTHWEST TERRITORIES TERRITOIRES DU NORD-OUEST | 13. ☐ NUNAVUT NUNAVUT | |

If other please specify/
Si autre, veuillez préciser

This information is being collected under the authority of The Corporations Information Act for the purpose of maintaining a public data base of corporate information.
La Loi sur les renseignements exigés des personnes morales autorise la collecte de ces renseignements pour constituer une banque de données accessible au public.

07201(08/99)   FOR MINISTRY USE ONLY/À L'USAGE DU MINISTÈRE   ☐ See deficiency letter enclosed/Voir l'avis d'insuffisance ci-joint

200

FORM 2 - EXTRA PROVINCIAL CORPORATIONS/
FORMULE 2 - PERSONNES MORALES EXTRA-PROVINCIALES
Please type or print all information in block capital letters using black ink.
Prière de dactylographier les renseignements ou de les écrire en caractères d'imprimerie à l'encre noire.

FOR MINISTRY USE ONLY À L'USAGE DU MINISTÈRE SEULEMENT	Ontario Corporation Number/ Numéro matricule de la personne morale en Ontario	Date of Incorporation or Amalgamation Date de constitution ou fusion Year/Année Month/Mois Day/Jour	For Ministry Use Only À l'usage du ministère seulement

12. Name and Office Address of the Chief Officer/Manager in Ontario/
Nom et adresse du bureau du directeur général/gérant en Ontario   ☐ Not Applicable/Ne s'applique pas

Last Name/Nom de famille   First Name/Prénom   Middle Name/Autres prénoms

Street Number/Numéro civique

Street Name/Nom de la rue

Street Name (cont'd)/Nom de la rue (suite)   Suite/Bureau

City/Town/Ville   Postal Code/Code postal

ONTARIO, CANADA

Date Effective
Date d'entrée en vigueur   Year/Année Month/Mois Day/Jour   Date Ceased Date de cessation des fonctions   Year/Année Month/Mois Day/Jour

13. Name and Office Address of Agent for Service in Ontario - Check One box
Nom et adresse du bureau du mandataire aux fins de signification en Ontario. Cocher la case pertinente.

☐ Not Applicable/Ne s'applique pas

Only applies to foreign business corporations S'applique seulement aux personnes morales étrangères

a) ☐ Individual or un particulier ou   b) ☐ Corporation une personne morale
Complete appropriate sections below/Remplir les parties pertinentes ci-dessous.

a) Individual Name/Nom du particulier

Last Name/Nom de famille   First Name/Prénom   Middle Name/Autres prénoms

b) Ontario Corporation Number/Numéro matricule de la personne morale en Ontario

Corporation Name including punctuation/Raison sociale, y compris la ponctuation

c) Address/Adresse

c/o / a/s

Street Number/Numéro civique   Street Name/Nom de la rue   Suite/Bureau

Street Name (cont'd)/Nom de la rue (suite)   City/Town/Ville

ONTARIO, CANADA   Postal Code/Code postal

14.
(Print or type name in full of the person authorizing filing / Dactylographier ou inscrire le prénom et le nom en caractères d'imprimerie de la personne qui autorise l'enregistrement)

I/Je

certify that the information set out herein, is true and correct.
atteste que les renseignements précités sont véridiques et exacts.

Check appropriate box
Cocher la case pertinente

D) ☐ Director/Administrateur

O) ☐ Officer /Dirigeant

P) ☐ Other individual having knowledge of the affairs of the Corporation/Autre personne ayant connaissance des activités de la personne morale

NOTE/REMARQUE: Sections 13 and 14 of the **Corporations Information Act** provide penalties for making false or misleading statements or omissions. Les articles 13 et 14 de la **Loi sur les renseignements exigés des personnes morales** prévoient des peines en cas de déclaration fausse ou trompeuse, ou d'omission.

This information is being collected under the authority of The Corporations Information Act for the purpose of maintaining a public data base of corporate information.
La Loi sur les renseignements exigés des personnes morales autorise la collecte de ces renseignements pour constituer une banque de données accessible au public.

07201 (08/99) FOR MINISTRY USE ONLY/À L'USAGE DU MINISTÈRE   ☐ See deficiency letter enclosed/Voir l'avis d'insuffisance ci-joint

Prince Edward Island

CANADA

APPLICATION FOR LICENSE OR REGISTRATION CERTIFICATE

under

The Licensing Act

(a) Name of Corporation . . . .

(b) Address of head office, if corporation . . . .

. . . .

(c) Address and occupation, if individual applicant . . . .

. . . .

(d) If partnership, name and address of partners: . . . .

. . . .

. . . .

. . . .

(e) Jurisdiction of Incorporation . . . .

. . . .

(f) Nature of business carried on by applicant . . . .

. . . .

. . . .

(g) Address of applicant's principal place of business in Prince Edward Island (if applicable)

. . . .

. . . .

. . . .

. . . .

(h) Number of branches operated by applicant in Prince Edward Island, with location of each branch (if

applicable) . . . .

. . . .

. . . .

. . . .

The above named applicant hereby declares that the information herein furnished is correct and accurate, and applies for license or registration certificate under the provisions of the Statute of Prince Edward Island.

Dated at . . . . this . . . . day of . . . . A.D. 20 . . . .

Corporate Section
Consumer, Corporate and Insurance Services
Province of Prince Edward Island
PO Box 2000
Charlottetown. PE C1A 7N8   . . . .
Tel. (902) 368-4550   **Signature of applicant**

203

Saskatchewan Justice
Corporations
Branch

Application for Registration
Form 22
The Business Corporations Act

1.	Name of entity:	Corp. # in home jurisdiction

2. Address of Registered Office in home jurisdiction:

Street Address

Name of City/Town/Village	Province	Postal Code

3.	Corporate history:	Fundamental changes since Incorporation/Amalgamation in home jurisdiction (E.g. Name changes & date of change, etc.) – Attach an additional sheet if insufficient space.
	Incorporation/Amalgamation Date in home jurisdiction:	
	Jurisdiction of Incorporation/Amalgamation:	

4. The directors of the corporation are: (Attach an additional sheet if insufficient space)

Name	Address	Position held (if any)

5. Attached documents include:
   - Power of Attorney
   - Certificate of Status (or Compliance) from home jurisdiction

I _____, being _____ of the
(Director/Solicitor and Agent/Authorized Officer)

corporation, certify that the Application for Registration and any attachments are correct and that I have the authority to request this Application be filed pursuant to *The Business Corporations Act*.

Date: _____ Signature: _____

**Saskatchewan
Justice**
Corporations
Branch

Articles of Incorporation
Form 1
The Business Corporations Act

---

1.   **Name of corporation** (print or type the name of your corporation):

2.   **The classes and any maximum number of shares that the corporation is authorized to issue.** (If there is to be more than one class of shares indicate all rights attached to each class OR attach a separate sheet indicating the rights attached to each class):

3.   **Restrictions, if any, on share transfers:**

4.   **Authorized number of directors** (minimum and maximum or fixed):

5.   **Restrictions, if any, on businesses the corporation may carry on or on powers the corporation may exercise:**

6.   **Other provisions, if any:**

Incorporator (must be completed in full):

Name: _____

Address: _____

_____

Date: _____ **Signature:** _____

Rev. 11/99

Saskatchewan Justice
Corporations Branch

Business Name Registration
Form A
The Business Names Registration Act

☐ Sole Proprietor   ☐ Partnership   ☐ Joint Venture   ☐ Syndicate

Please print (or type) clearly

1. **Name of Business:** _____

2. **Location of Business:** _____
    (a box number is not acceptable)

    _____
    City, Town, Village or Rural Municipality (name and number)   Prov.   Postal Code

3. **Mailing Address:**   ☐ Same as Above   **OR**

    _____
    Street Address or Box Number

    _____
    City, Town or Village   Prov.   Postal Code

4. **I/We,**

a) **Do hereby declare that** (Please check only **ONE** box)

☐ I am / We are carrying on business in Saskatchewan.   ☐ I / We intend to carry on business in Saskatchewan.

b) **No other individual or corporation is a member of this firm.**

(Full name, residential address and Postal Code for all individual registrants of this name. If registrant is a corporation, name and entity number are required.)

Date	Last Name, First Name, Middle Name or Initials	Residential Address (for individuals only – Entity Number for Corporations)	Signature of Individual (In case of Corporation – Signature of Director / Solicitor and Agent / Authorized Officer)

Rev. 01/00

206

 **Saskatchewan**
Justice
Corporations
Branch

Initial Notice of Registered Office
Form 3.1
The Business Corporations Act

1.

Location of registered office
• This is where the books of the corporation are held.
• Must not be a box number.
• May be a legal land description (including R.M. name and number).
• Must be located in Saskatchewan.

_____

Street Address (or legal land description, including R.M. name and number)

_____   **Saskatchewan**   _____

Name of City/Town/Village   Postal Code

2.

Mailing address of registered office, including postal code
(If the mailing address is the same as the Registered Office, check the box, otherwise, indicate the mailing address).
A box number is acceptable as a mailing address.

☐ Same as above   **OR**

_____

Street Address or Post Office box number

_____   _____   _____

Name of City/Town/Village   Province   Postal Code

Attention: _____ Phone (optional): _____

Rev. 11/99

Glossary of useful terms

A-De

Articles of Amendment
A document which must be filed with the government to make binding any alteration in the original Articles of Incorporation., i.e., to change the business purpose.

Articles of Incorporation
Documents filed with the Director of Companies branch to establish a legal corporation.

Assets
Anything owned with monetary value. This includes both real and personal property.

Authorized shares
The number of shares a corporation is authorized to sell.

Business number (BN)
The nine digit number which is assigned to your business by Revenue Canada.

Bylaws
Rules adopted by the corporation itself for the regulation of a corporation's own actions.

Calendar year
The accounting year beginning January 1 and ending on December 31.

CCP
Canadian Pension Plan

Certificate of Incorporation
The document issued by the government that creates a corporation according to the laws of the government. This may also have to be filed and approved by the provincial government.

Common stock
A class of stock, usually with voting rights, issued by a corporation which represents a specified share of ownership in the corporation.

Cooperative
A special type of corporation which is organized, owned, and controlled by members who join together for a common benefit.

Corporate designation
The final part of the business name which identifies a corporation. i.e. Corporation, Limited, etc.

Corporate purpose
The objective of the business. This statement is contained in the Articles of Incorporation.

Default rules
Statutory rules that take effect in the absence of contrary provisions in an Operating Agreement.

Descriptive element
The second part of a corporate name which implies the type of business the corporation is engaged in.

Di-Prov

Director

A person who has been chosen or elected by the shareholders to direct the actions of a corporation.

Dissolution

Formal statutory liquidation, termination and winding up of a business entity.

Distinctive element

The first part of a corporate name which will separate it from other similar companies.

Distribution

Payment of cash or property to a member, shareholder or partner according to his or her percentage of ownership.

Double taxation

Occurs when corporations pay tax on corporate profits and shareholders pay income tax on dividend or distributive income.

Extra-provincial

A business which is licensed or registered in another province.

Fictitious business name

A name other than the corporate name under which a corporation may do business as long as it is not used for fraudulent purposes. Also called a d/b/a/ (doing business as) name.

Fiscal year

Any 12-month period used by a business as its accounting period. Such accounting period may, for example, run from July 1 of one year through June 30 of the next year.

Foreign corporation

A corporation formed in one province but conducts some or all of its business in another province.

Free transfer of interests

The ability to transfer ownership to a non-member without the consent of the other members of the corporation.

Incorporator

A person who signs the Articles of Incorporation upon petitioning the province for a corporate charter.

Minority stockholder

One who owns or controls less than 50 percent of the stock in a corporation.

Minutes

Written records of formal proceedings of stockholders' and directors' meetings.

NUANS

A federally-based name search service which is preferred throughout Canada.

No-par value stock

Shares of stock without specified value.

Not-for-profit corporation

A corporation organized for some charitable, civil, social or other purpose that does not entail the generation of profit or the distribution of its income to members, principals, shareholders, officers or others affiliated with it. Such corporations are accorded special treatment under the law.

Parliamentary procedure

Rules, such as "Roberts Rules of Order," which govern stockholders' meetings, directors' meetings, etc.

Par value stock

Shares of stock with a specified value.

Provincial statutes

Laws created by a provincial legislature.

Prox-T

Proxy

Authorization by a stockholder allowing another to vote his shares of stock.

Publicly owned corporation

One whose stock is owned by more than 25 stockholders and is regulated by the government.

Quorum

A majority of the stockholders or directors necessary for vote-counting and decision-making at a meeting. A quorum may consist of a greater number than a simple majority if stated in the bylaws.

Resolution

Decisions of the directors which affect the course of business and operations of the corporation.

Share

A certificate stipulating a specified unit of ownership.

Shareholder

See Stockholder.

Start-up venture

A new business having no track record.

Statutory agent

A corporation or individual who assumes the legal responsibility for receiving mail and accepting legal service for the corporation.

Stock certificate

Written instrument evidencing a share in the ownership of a corporation.

Stockholder

A holder of one or more shares of the stock of a corporation. A stockholder may be called a "shareholder."

Subsidiary

A corporation owned by another corporation.

Trade name

Any name by which a company identifies itself. It may be an actual name or a fictitious name.

Index